Undergraduate Topics in Computer Science

Undergraduate Topics in Computer Science (UTiCS) delivers high-quality instructional content for undergraduates studying in all areas of computing and information science. From core foundational and theoretical material to final-year topics and applications, UTiCS books take a fresh, concise, and modern approach and are ideal for self-study or for a one- or two-semester course. The texts are all authored by established experts in their fields, reviewed by an international advisory board, and contain numerous examples and problems. Many include fully worked solutions.

For further volumes:
http://www.springer.com/series/7592

Maribel Fernández

Models
of Computation

An Introduction
to Computability Theory

 Springer

Dr. Maribel Fernández
King's College London
UK

ISSN 1863-7310
ISBN 978-1-84882-433-1   e-ISBN 978-1-84882-434-8
DOI 10.1007/978-1-84882-434-8
Springer Dordrecht Heidelberg London New York

British Library Cataloguing in Publication Data
A catalogue record for this book is available from the British Library

Library of Congress Control Number: Applied for

Springer is part of Springer Science+Business Media (www.springer.com)

Preface

Aim

The aim of this book is to provide an introduction to essential concepts in computability, presenting and comparing alternative models of computation. We define and analyse the most significant models of computation and their associated programming paradigms, from Turing machines to the emergent computation models inspired by systems biology and quantum physics.

About this book

This book provides an introduction to computability using a series of abstract models of computation.

After giving the historical context and the original challenges that motivated the development of computability theory in the 1930s, we start reviewing the traditional models of computation: Turing machines, Church's Lambda calculus (or λ-calculus), and the theory of recursive functions of Gödel and Kleene. These three models of computation are equivalent in the sense that any computation procedure that can be expressed in one of them can also be expressed in the others. Indeed, Church's Thesis states that the set of computable functions is exactly the set of functions that can be defined in these models.

Each of the above-mentioned models of computation gave rise to a programming paradigm: imperative, functional, or algebraic. We also include in the first part of the book a computation model based on deduction in a fragment of first-order logic, which gave rise to the logic programming paradigm, because the work by Herbrand in this area dates also from the late 1920s and early 1930s.

As programming languages evolved and new programming techniques were developed, other models of computation became available; for instance, based on the concept of object or on a notion of interaction between agents. It is possible, for example, to show that any computable function can be defined by using an abstract device where one can define objects, invoke their methods, and update them. In the second part of the book, we describe a calculus of objects as a foundation for object-oriented programming and compare its computational power with the traditional ones. We also describe a graphical, interaction-based model of computation and a formalism for the specification of concurrent computations.

Recently, there has been a renewed interest in computability theory, with the emergence of several models of computation inspired by biological and physical processes. In the last chapter of the book, we discuss biologically inspired calculi and quantum computing.

This book is addressed to advanced undergraduate students, as a complement to programming languages or computability courses, and to postgraduate students who are interested in the theory of computation. It was developed to accompany lectures in a Master's course on models of computation at King's College London. The book is for the most part self-contained; only some basic knowledge of logic is assumed. Basic programming skills in one language are useful, and knowledge of more programming languages will be helpful but is not necessary.

Each chapter includes exercises that provide an opportunity to apply the concepts and techniques presented. Answers to selected exercises are given at the end of the book. Although some of the questions are just introductory, most exercises are designed with the goal of testing the *understanding* of the subject; for instance, by requiring the student to adapt a given technique to different contexts.

Organisation

The book is organised as follows. Chapter 1 gives an introduction to computability and provides background material for the rest of the book, which is organised into two parts.

In Part I, we present the traditional models of computation. We start with the study of various classes of automata in Chapter 2. These are abstract machines defined by a collection of states and a transition function that controls the way the machine's state changes. Depending on the type of memory and the kind of response that the automaton can give to external signals, we obtain machines with different computation power. After giving an informal description, we provide formal specifications and examples of finite automata, push-down automata, and Turing machines. The chapter ends with a discussion of the applications of these automata to programming language design and implementation.

The next two chapters are dedicated to the study of computation models inspired by the idea of "computation as functional transformation". In Chapter 3, we give an overview of the λ-calculus, with examples that demonstrate the power of this formalism, highlighting the role of the λ-calculus as a foundation for the functional programming paradigm. In Chapter 4, we define primitive recursion and the general class of partial recursive functions.

The final chapter in Part I describes a model of computation based on deduction in a fragment of first-order logic. We introduce the Principle of Resolution and the notion of unification. We then study the link between these results and the development of logic programming languages based on SLD-resolution.

Part II studies three modern computation paradigms that can be seen as the foundation of three well-known programming styles: object-oriented, interaction-based, and concurrent programming, respectively. In addition, it includes a short discussion on emergent models of computation inspired by biological and physical processes. More precisely, Part II is organised as follows.

In Chapter 6, we analyse the process of computation from an object-oriented perspective: Computation is structured around objects that own a collection of functions (methods in the object-oriented terminology). We describe object-oriented computation models, providing examples and a comparison with traditional models of computation.

In Chapter 7, we study graphical models of computation, where computation is centred on the notion of interaction. Programs are collections of agents that interact to produce a result. We show that some graphical models naturally induce a notion of sequentiality, whereas others can be used to describe parallel functions.

Chapter 8 describes a calculus of communicating processes that can be used to specify concurrent computation systems, and gives a brief account of an alternative view of concurrency inspired by a chemical metaphor.

Chapter 9 gives a short introduction to some of the emergent models of computation: biologically inspired calculi and quantum computing.

The last chapter of the book (Chapter 10) contains answers to a selection of exercises.

At the end of the book there is a bibliographical section with references to articles and books where the interested reader can find more information.

Acknowledgements

The material presented in this book has been prepared using several different sources, including the references mentioned above and notes for my courses in London, Paris, and Montevideo. I would like to thank the reviewers, the editors, and the students in the Department of Computer Science at King's College London for their comments on previous versions of the book, and my family for their continuous support.

Maribel Fernández
London, November 2008

Contents

Part II. Modern Models of Computation

1

Introduction

This book is concerned with abstract models of computation. Several new models of computation have emerged in the last few years (e.g., chemical machines, bio-computing, quantum computing, etc.). Also, many developments in traditional computational models have been proposed with the aim of taking into account the new demands of computer system users and the new capabilities of computation engines. A new model of computation, or a new feature in a traditional one, usually is reflected in a new family of programming languages and new paradigms of software development. Thus, an understanding of the traditional and emergent models of computation facilitates the use of modern programming languages and software development tools, informs the choice of the correct language for a given application, and is essential for the design of new programming languages.

But what exactly is a "model of computation"? To understand what is meant by a model of computation, we briefly recall a little history. The notions of computability and computable functions go back a long time. The ancient Greeks and the Egyptians, for instance, had a good understanding of computation "methods". The Persian scientist Al-Khwarizmi in 825 wrote a book entitled "On the Calculation with Hindu Numerals", which contained the description of several procedures that could now be called algorithms. His name appears to be the origin of the word "algorithm": When his book was translated into Latin, its title was changed to "Algoritmi de Numero Indorum". The word "algorithm" was later used to name the class of computation procedures described in the book. Roughly, an *algorithm* is:

− a finite description of a computation in terms of well-defined elementary operations (or instructions);

− a deterministic procedure: the next step is uniquely defined, if there is one;

− a method that always produces a result, no matter what the input is (that is, the computation described by an algorithm always terminates).

The modern computability theory has its roots in the work done at the beginning of the twentieth century to formalise the concept of an "algorithm" without referring to a specific programming language or physical computational device. A computation model abstracts away from the material details of the device we are using to make the calculations, be it an abacus, pen and paper, or our favourite programming language and processor.

In the 1930s, logicians (in particular Alan Turing and Alonzo Church) studied the meaning of computation as an abstract mental process and started to design theoretical devices to model the process of computation, which could be used to express algorithms and also non-terminating computations.

The notion of a *partial function* generalises the notion of an algorithm described above by considering computation processes that do not always lead to a result. Indeed, some expressions do not have a value:

1. $True + 4$ is not defined (we cannot add a number and a Boolean).

2. $10/0$ is not defined.

3. The expression factorial(-1) does not have a value if factorial is a recursive function defined as follows:

$$\begin{aligned} \text{factorial}(0) &= 1 \\ \text{factorial}(n) &= n * \text{factorial}(n-1) \end{aligned}$$

The first is a type error since addition is a function from numbers to numbers: For any pair of natural numbers, the result of the addition is defined. We say that addition is a *total function* on the natural numbers.

The second is a different kind of problem: 10 and 0 are numbers, but division by 0 is not defined. We say that division is a *partial function* on the natural numbers.

There is another case in which an expression may not have a value: The computation may loop, as in the third example above. We will say that factorial is a *partial function* on the integers.

The notion of a partial function is so essential in computability theory that it deserves to be our first definition.

Definition 1.1 (Partial function)

Let A and B be sets. We denote their Cartesian product by $A \times B$; that is, $A \times B$ denotes the set of all the pairs where the first element is in A and the second in B. We use the symbol $\in$ to denote membership; i.e., we write $a \in A$ to indicate that the element a is in the set A.

A *partial function* f from A to B (abbreviated as $f : A \to B$) is a subset of $A \times B$ such that if $(x, y) \in f$ and $(x, z) \in f$, then $y = z$. In other words, a partial function from A to B associates to each element of A at most one element of B.

If $(x, y) \in f$, we write $f(x) = y$ and say that y is the *image* of x. The elements of A that have an image in B are in the *domain* of f.

In the study of computability, we are often interested only in functions whose domain and co-domain are the set of integer numbers. In some cases, this is even restricted to natural numbers; that is, integers that are positive or zero.

The notion of a partial function is also important in modern programming techniques. From an abstract point of view, we can say that *each program defines a partial function*. In practice, we are interested in more than the function that the program computes; we also want to know how the function is computed, how efficient the computation is, how much memory space we will need, etc. However, in this book we will concentrate on whether a problem has a computable solution or not, and how the actual computation mechanism is expressed, without trying to obtain the most efficient computation.

1.1 Models of computation

Some mathematical functions are computable and some are not: There are problems for which no computer program can provide a solution even assuming that the amount of time and space available to carry out the computation is infinite. Complexity theory studies the "practical" aspects of computability; that is, for a computable function, it answers the question: How much time and space will be needed for the computation? We will not cover complexity theory in this book but instead will concentrate on computability.

First we need to define precisely the notion of a computable function. This is a difficult task and is still the subject of research. We will first give an intuitive definition.

Definition 1.2 (Computable function)

All the functions on the natural numbers that can be effectively computed in an ideal world, where time and space are unlimited, are called *partial recursive functions* or *computable functions*.

The definition of a computable function above does not say what our notion of "effective" computation is: Which programming language is used to define the function? What kind of device is used to compute it? We need a *model of computation* to abstract away from the material details of the programming language and the processor we are using. In fact, computability was studied as a branch of mathematical logic well before programming languages and computers were built. Three well-studied abstract models of computation dating from the 1930s are

— *Turing machines*, designed by Alan Turing to provide a formalisation of the concept of an algorithm;

— the *Lambda calculus*, designed by Alonzo Church with the aim of providing a foundation for mathematics based on the notion of a function; and

— the *theory of recursive functions*, first outlined by Kurt Gödel and further developed by Stephen Kleene.

These three models of computation are equivalent in that they can all express the same class of functions. Indeed, *Church's Thesis* says that they compute all the so-called computable functions. More generally, Church's Thesis says that the *same* class of functions on the integers can be computed in any sequential, universal model of computation that satisfies basic postulates about determinism and the effectiveness of elementary computation steps. This class of *computable functions* is the set of partial recursive functions.

We say that a programming language is *Turing complete* if any computable function can be written in this language. All general-purpose programming languages available nowadays are complete in this sense. Turing completeness is usually proved through an encoding in the programming language of a standard universal computation model.

1.2 Some non-computable functions

Since the 1930s, it has been known that certain basic problems cannot be solved by computation. The typical example is the Halting problem discussed below, which was proved to be non-computable by Church and Turing. Other examples of non-computable problems are:

— Hilbert's 10th problem: solving Diophantine equations.

Diophantine equations are equations of the form

$$P(x_1, \ldots, x_n) = Q(x_1, \ldots, x_n)$$

where P and Q are polynomials with integer coefficients. A polynomial is a sum of monomials, each monomial being a product of variables with a coefficient. The coefficients are constants; for example, $x^2 + 2x + 1$ is a polynomial on one variable, x.

The mathematician David Hilbert asked for an algorithm to solve Diophantine equations; that is, an algorithm that takes a Diophantine equation as input and determines whether this equation has integer solutions or not. This problem was posed by Hilbert in 1900 in a list of open problems presented at the International Congress of Mathematicians, and it became known as Hilbert's 10th problem. It is important to note that the coefficients of the polynomials are integers and the solution requested is an assignment of integer numbers to the variables in the equation.

Hilbert's 10th problem remained open until 1970, when it was shown to be undecidable in general by Yuri Matijasevič, Julia Robinson, Martin Davis, and Hilary Putnam.

— Hilbert's *decision problem*: the *Entscheidungsproblem*.

This problem was also posed by Hilbert in 1900. Briefly, the problem requires writing an algorithm to decide whether any given mathematical assertion in the functional calculus is provable.

Hilbert thought that this problem was computable, but his conjecture was proved wrong by Church and Turing, who showed that an algorithm to solve this problem could also solve the Halting problem.

These are examples of *undecidable problems*. We end this introduction with a description of the Halting problem.

The Halting problem.   Intuitively, to solve the Halting problem, we need an algorithm that can check whether a given program will stop or not on a given input. More precisely, the problem is formulated as follows:

Write an algorithm H such that given

— the description of an algorithm A (which requires one input) and

— an input I,

H will return 1 if A stops with the input I and 0 if A does not stop on I.

We can see the algorithm H as a function: $H(A, I) = 1$ if the program A stops when the input I is provided, and $H(A, I) = 0$ otherwise.

In the quest for a solution to this problem, Turing and Church constructed two abstract models of computation that later became the basis of the modern theory of computing: Turing machines and the Lambda calculus.

In fact, Church and Turing proved that there is no algorithm H such that, for any pair (A, I) as described above, H produces the required output. Its proof, which follows, is short and elegant.

Proof

If there were such an H, we could use it to define the following program C:

C takes as input an algorithm A and computes H(A, A). If the result is 0, then it answers 1 and stops; otherwise it loops forever.

Below we will use the notation $A(I)\uparrow$, where A is a program and I is its input, to represent the fact that the program A does not stop on the input I. Using the program C, for any program A, the following properties hold:

– If $H(A, A) = 1$, then $C(A)\uparrow$ and $A(A)$ stops.

– If $H(A, A) = 0$, then $C(A)$ stops and $A(A)\uparrow$.

In other words, $C(A)$ stops if and only if $A(A)$ does not stop.

Since A is arbitrary, it could be C itself, and then we obtain a contradiction:

$C(C)$ stops if and only if $C(C)$ does not stop.

Therefore H cannot exist.

□

The proofs of undecidability of Hilbert's decision problem or Diophantine equations are more involved and we will not show them in this book, but it is important to highlight that these results, obtained with the help of abstract models of computation, still apply to current computers.

Since the class of computable functions is the same for all the traditional computation models, we deduce that imperative or functional languages (which are based on Turing machines and the Lambda calculus, respectively) can describe exactly the same class of computable functions. Several other models of computation, or idealised computers, have been proposed, some of them inspired by advances in physics, chemistry, and biology. There is hope that some of these new models might solve some outstanding non-feasible problems (i.e., problems that cannot be solved on a realistic timescale in traditional models).

1.3 Further reading

Readers interested in algorithms can find more information in Harel and Feldman's book [22]. Further information on partial functions and computability in general can be found in [47, 49] and in the chapter on computability in Mitchell's book [36]. Additional references are provided in the following chapters.

1.4 Exercises

1. Give more examples of total and partial functions on natural numbers.

2. To test whether a number is even or odd, a student has designed the following function:

   $$\text{test}(x) \overset{\text{def}}{=} \quad \text{if } x = 0 \text{ then "even"}$$
   $$\text{else if } x = 1 \text{ then "odd" else test}(x-2)$$

   Is this a total function on the set of integer numbers? Is it total on the natural numbers?

3. Consider the following variant of the Halting problem:

   Write an algorithm H such that, given the description of an algorithm A that requires one input, H will return 1 if A stops for any input I and H will return 0 if there is at least one input I for which A does not stop.

   In other words, the algorithm H should read the description of A and decide whether it stops for all its possible inputs or there is at least one input for which A does not stop.

   Show that this version of the Halting problem is also undecidable.

Part I

Traditional Models of Computation

2

Automata and Turing Machines

In the 1930s, logicians (in particular Alan Turing and Alonzo Church) studied the meaning of computation as an abstract mental process and started to design theoretical devices to model it. As mentioned in the introduction, they needed a precise, formal definition of an algorithm in order to show that some of the problems posed by David Hilbert at the 1900 International Congress of Mathematicians could not be solved algorithmically. This was a very important step towards the construction of actual computers and, later, the design of programming languages. Turing machines influenced the development of digital computers, and the Lambda calculus is the basis of functional programming languages. At the same time, computers give to the early computability studies a practical application.

Turing defined an algorithm as a process that an abstract machine, now called a Turing machine, can perform. Church described his algorithms using the Lambda calculus. Several other models of computation, or idealised computers, have been proposed and studied since then. Depending on the features of the idealised computer, some abstract models of computation can represent all computable functions and others cannot. For instance, finite automata, one of the classes of machines that we will define in this chapter, have less computation power than Turing machines but are very useful in text processing and in the lexical analysis phase of compilers and interpreters. Another model of computation, called a push-down automaton, is used in parsing (the second phase of compilers and interpreters); it is a generalisation of the finite automaton that includes memory in the form of a stack. These two models of computation are not Turing complete; that is, they are not powerful enough to express all the computable functions. The Turing machine is a more general automaton that includes an unlimited memory.

In this chapter, we will define and compare these three kinds of automata from the point of view of their power to represent algorithms. But first we will discuss another application of these machines: We can associate to each automaton a *formal language*, which is simply the set of sequences of signals that will take the machine to a specific state (a *final state*). We call this set of sequences the language *recognised* by the automaton. Each of the classes of automata mentioned above can recognise a different class of *formal* language.

2.1 Formal languages and automata

Formal languages are a particular kind of language that we distinguish from, for instance, *natural languages* such as French, English, Spanish, etc. A formal language is a set of *words* with a given *syntax* (the rules that govern the construction of words) and a *semantics* that gives meaning to the words.

First, we need to specify what we mean by "word". Formally, we start by fixing the *alphabet* of the language. This is just a finite set $\mathcal{X}$ of symbols.

Definition 2.1 (Language)

A formal language, or simply a language, with alphabet $\mathcal{X}$ is a set of words over $\mathcal{X}$.

A *word* over $\mathcal{X}$ is a sequence of symbols taken from $\mathcal{X}$; that is, a *chain* or string of elements in $\mathcal{X}$. The chain could be empty, in which case we will write it ϵ.

For example, a programming language such as Java or Haskell is a formal language. It has well-defined syntax rules; for instance, to build a conditional expression, we use the string "if" followed by a condition, etc.

Once we have defined the alphabet and the set of words in the language, two questions arise: How do we check that a given word belongs to the language? How do we generate the words in the language? To answer these questions, we will build abstract machines — the *automata* mentioned above.

It is clear that the problem of deciding whether a word belongs to a certain language or not can be more or less difficult depending on the form of the language. In the 1950s, the linguist Noam Chomsky classified formal languages into four categories according to their expressive power. The first two classes of languages, called *regular* and *context-free*, respectively, are useful to describe the syntax of programming languages. The fourth, most general class of languages has all the expressive power of Turing machines. For each class of language in Chomsky's hierarchy, there is an associated class of automata. The simplest kind, used to recognise regular languages, are called *finite automata*; they are useful to describe the lower-level syntactic units of a programming language, and for this reason we find them in most compilers (lexical analysers are specified as finite automata). To analyse the syntactic structure of a program, we need more than a finite automaton: To recognise context-free languages, we use *push-down automata*.

We study finite automata in the next section. We then go on to define push-down automata before giving a description of Turing machines.

2.2 Finite automata

Automata can be seen as *abstract machines*, or abstract models of computation. Finite automata are the simplest kind of machines in this family, and the computations that they can make are very restricted. However, they have important applications (for instance, in lexical analysis, as mentioned above), and because of their simplicity they are a useful tool for the study of algorithms.

Finite automata are machines that can be in a finite number of different states and that respond to external signals by performing a *transition*; that is, a change of state (they can also output a message).

Example 2.2

A lift can be modelled as a finite automaton. It can be in a finite number of different states (corresponding to its position, the direction in which it is going, whether the door is closed or open, etc.) and reacts to external signals.

Another example is an automatic door (for instance, the doors at the entrance of an airport hall). They can be in a finite number of states (open or closed) and react to signals (sent when somebody stands near the door).

A finite automaton with alphabet $\mathcal{X}$ is defined by a finite number of states and a set of transitions between states (one transition for each symbol in $\mathcal{X}$). There is a distinguished state, called the *initial* state, where the automaton starts, and one or several *final states*, or accepting states.

A finite automaton can be represented in different ways; we will often use a graphical representation, which emphasises the fact that automata are transition machines. However, before giving the graphical representation, we will give a formal and concise definition of a finite automaton.

Definition 2.3 (Finite automaton)

A finite automaton is a tuple $(\mathcal{X}, Q, q_0, F, \delta)$, where

1. $\mathcal{X}$ is an alphabet (that is, a set of symbols);

2. Q is a finite set of states $\{q_0, \ldots, q_n\}$ for some $n \geq 0$;

3. $q_0 \in Q$ is the initial state;

4. $F \subseteq Q$ is the subset of final states; and

5. δ is the transition function $\delta : Q \times \mathcal{X} \to Q$.

We can better visualise this definition if we give the transition function as a diagram where the states are represented by points (or circles) and the change of state (i.e., transition) is represented by an arrow. In other words, the transition function is represented by edges between nodes in a graph. From this point of view, a finite automaton is a directed graph, where the nodes represent states and an edge from q_i to q_j labelled by $x \in \mathcal{X}$ represents a transition $\delta(q_i, x) = q_j$.

Example 2.4

The automaton $\mathcal{A} = (\{a\}, \{q_0, q_1\}, q_0, \{q_0\}, \delta)$, where $\delta(q_0, a) = q_1$ and $\delta(q_1, a) = q_0$, is represented by

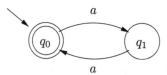

The arrow indicates the initial state (q_0), and the double circle denotes a final state (in this case, the initial state is also final).

Another image, depicted in Figure 2.1, can help us see automata as machines with

− a control unit (states and transition function) and

− a tape with symbols from the alphabet.

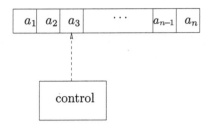

Figure 2.1   A finite automaton depicted as a machine.

The machine is in the initial state at the beginning, with the reading head in the first position of the tape. It reads a symbol on the tape (or receives an external signal), moves to the next symbol, and makes a state transition according to the symbol just read. This cycle is repeated until we reach a final state or the end of the tape.

The language associated with a finite automaton — sometimes referred to as the language *recognised* by the automaton — is simply the set of words (or sequences of signals) that takes it to a final state.

Definition 2.5

A word w over the alphabet $\mathcal{X}$ is *recognised*, or *accepted*, by a finite automaton with alphabet $\mathcal{X}$ if the machine described above reaches a final state when started in the initial state on a tape that contains the word w and such that the reading head is positioned on the first symbol of w.

Using our graphical description of automata, we could reformulate the definition of recognised words by saying that a word w over $\mathcal{X}$ is recognised by an automaton with alphabet $\mathcal{X}$ if there is a path from the initial state to a final state in the graph that represents the automaton such that all the edges in the path are labelled by the symbols in the word w (in the same order).

Example 2.6

All the words that contain an even number of symbols a (that is, all the words of the form $(a)^{2n}$, where n can also be zero) are recognised by the automaton given in Example 2.4.

Definition 2.7

The *language recognised* by an automaton $\mathcal{A}$ is the set of words that the automaton accepts; we will denote it by $L(\mathcal{A})$.

Lexical analysers are often specified using finite automata; we give a simple example below.

Example 2.8

Consider a programming language where the syntax rules specify that identifiers must be finite sequences of letters or numbers (capitals, punctuation symbols, and other characters are not allowed), starting with a letter. We can use the following automaton to recognise strings satisfying the constraints (an arrow labelled by $a \ldots z$ represents a set of arrows, each labelled with one of the letters a to z, and similarly an arrow labelled with $0 \ldots 9$ is an abbreviation for a set of arrows, each labelled with a digit).

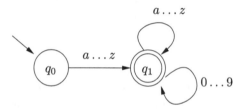

2.2.1 Deterministic and non-deterministic automata

We defined finite automata using a transition *function* $\delta : Q \times \mathcal{X} \to Q$. Thus, given a state and an input, the next state is uniquely determined — we say that the automaton is *deterministic*.

We can generalise this using a relation $\delta \subseteq Q \times \mathcal{X} \times Q$ instead of a function. This means that δ is now defined as a set of triples, where the first and third elements are states and the second element is a symbol from the alphabet. The idea is that we may have several triples with the same first and second elements. For instance, if δ contains (q_i, x, q) and (q_i, x, q'), then from the state q_i with input x, either q or q' can be reached. Thus, given a state and an input, the automaton can move to a number of different states in a *non-deterministic* way. Another way to represent this relation is as a function from Q and $\mathcal{X}$ to the set of parts of Q:

$$\delta : Q \times \mathcal{X} \to \mathcal{P}(Q)$$

In this way, we can write $\delta(q, x)$ to denote all the states that can be reached from q when the machine reads the symbol x.

One may wonder what is the use of a machine that can make transitions in a non-deterministic way. Does this kind of behaviour have a computational meaning? Indeed, a non-deterministic automaton can be understood as a parallel machine: When there are several states that can be reached in a transition, we can think of this as several threads proceeding in parallel.

However, deterministic and non-deterministic finite automata have the same computation power. They are equivalent: They recognise exactly the same class of languages (or implement the same class of functions). This is not the case with more powerful automata. There are examples of machines for which the non-deterministic versions are strictly more powerful than the deterministic ones.

Non-deterministic finite automata can also be represented graphically. We will define them using graphs where nodes correspond to states and edges describe transitions, with the essential difference that now we can have several edges coming out from the same state and labelled by the same symbol.

Example 2.9

The non-deterministic automaton

$$\mathcal{A} = (\{a, b, c\}, \{q_0, q_1, q_2\}, q_0, \{q_1, q_2\}, \delta)$$

where $\delta(q_0, a) = \{q_1, q_2\}$, $\delta(q_1, b) = \{q_1\}$, and $\delta(q_2, c) = \{q_2\}$, is represented in Figure 2.2. We use the same conventions as above: The arrow points to the initial state, and a double circle indicates a final state; in this case we have two final states.

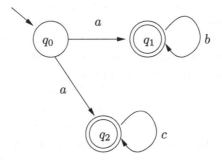

Figure 2.2 Diagram of the finite automaton $\mathcal{A}$

The language recognised by a non-deterministic automaton is defined in the same way as in the case of deterministic automata.

If $\mathcal{A} = (\mathcal{X}, Q, q_0, F, \delta)$ is a non-deterministic automaton, the language $L(\mathcal{A})$ recognised by $\mathcal{A}$ is the set of words over $\mathcal{X}$ such that there is a path in the graph representing the automaton $\mathcal{A}$ from the initial state to a final state, where each edge in the path is labelled by a symbol in the word.

The main difference with the previous definition is that we can now have several different paths labelled by the same word.

For example, the non-deterministic automaton in Figure 2.2 recognises all the words in the alphabet $\{a, b, c\}$ that consist of an a followed by either a string of b or a string of c.

2.2.2 The power of finite automata

Only the languages in the most basic class in Chomsky's hierarchy (that is, *regular* languages) can be recognised by finite automata (deterministic or non-deterministic). In practice, it would be useful to have a simple test to know, given a language, whether there is some finite automaton that recognises it. In this way we could know, for instance, how difficult it would be to implement an algorithm to recognise words in this language.

We can try to answer this question by studying the properties of the languages that can be recognised by finite automata. On the one hand, regular languages are closed under simple set operations, such as union and intersection. On the other hand, it is possible to characterise the languages that cannot be recognised by finite automata using the so-called Pumping Lemma. We can use these two kinds of properties to decide whether a certain language can or cannot be recognised by a finite automaton.

We will not study in detail the closure properties of regular languages; instead we finish this section with the Pumping Lemma. Before giving its formal statement, we will discuss the intuitive ideas behind this result.

Suppose that a certain language can be recognised by a finite, deterministic automaton $\mathcal{A}$ with n states. If we consider an input w with more than n symbols, it is obvious that, to recognise w, $\mathcal{A}$ will have to repeat at least one of its states. In other words, there must be a loop in the path representing the transitions associated with w. Assume $w = a_1 \ldots a_m$ (with $m > n$), and let a_i, a_j be the symbols in the first and last transitions in the loop (therefore $i \leq j$). As a direct consequence of this observation, we can eliminate from w the symbols $a_i \ldots a_j$ and still the word $w' = a_1 \ldots a_{i-1} a_{j+1} \ldots a_m$ will be recognised by $\mathcal{A}$.

Similarly, we could traverse the loop in the path several times, repeating this sequence of symbols. Let us write $(a_i \ldots a_j)^*$ to denote words containing 0 or more repetitions of the sequence of symbols $a_i \ldots a_j$. Thus, all the words of the form $a_1 \ldots a_{i-1}(a_i \ldots a_j)^* a_{j+1} \ldots a_m$ will also be recognised by $\mathcal{A}$.

Therefore, if we have a sufficiently long word $w \in L(\mathcal{A})$, where $\mathcal{A}$ is a finite automaton, we can always identify a segment near the beginning of the word, which we can repeat as many times as we want, and all the resulting words will also belong to $L(\mathcal{A})$. Using the same reasoning, if, given a language L and a word $w \in L$, there is no segment of w with the property described above, then we can deduce that L is *not* a regular language.

Formally, the Pumping Lemma is stated as follows.

Proposition 2.10 (Pumping Lemma)

Let L be a regular language. There exists a constant n such that if z is any given word in L with more than n symbols, then there are three words, u, v, and w, such that z can be written as the concatenation uvw, where

1. the length of uv is less than or equal to n,

2. the length of v is greater than or equal to 1, and

3. for any $i \geq 0$, $uv^i w \in L$, where v^i represents the word v repeated i times.

The Pumping Lemma indicates that finite automata have limited computation power. For instance, we can use the Pumping Lemma to show that the language of well-balanced brackets (that is, words where each open bracket has a corresponding closing bracket) cannot be recognised by a finite automaton. This is indeed a corollary. Suppose, by contradiction, that the language L of well-balanced brackets is regular, and take the word $(^n)^n$; that is, n open brackets followed by n closed brackets, where n is the constant mentioned in the Pumping Lemma. Now, using this lemma, we know that there are words u, v, and w such that $(^n)^n = uvw$, the length of uv is less than or equal to n, and v is not empty. Hence v is built out of open brackets only, and the Pumping Lemma says that $uv^i w \in L$ for all i. Thus, L contains words that do not have a well-balanced number of brackets, contradicting our assumptions.

Corollary 2.11

The language L containing all the words over the alphabet $\{(,)\}$ where each (has a corresponding) is not regular.

This corollary shows that to check the syntax of programs that contain arithmetic expressions, we need more than finite automata.

The Pumping Lemma can also be used to show that no finite automaton can recognise the language L of strings built out of 0s and 1s such that each word is formed by the concatenation of a string w and its reverse $\overline{w}$:

$$L = \{w\overline{w} \mid w \text{ is a string of 0s and 1s and } \overline{w} \text{ is its mirror image}\}$$

No finite automaton can be used to check whether a given word belongs to this language or not. To recognise this language, and also the language consisting of words with well-balanced brackets, we need more powerful machines, such as the push-down automata described in the next section.

2.3 Push-down automata

Push-down automata are a more general version of finite automata: They have an additional component — a *stack* — that provides additional memory. Thanks to this memory, push-down automata (or PDAs for short) can recognise some languages that finite automata cannot recognise; the class of languages associated with PDAs contains strictly the set of regular languages. Languages that can be recognised by push-down automata are called *context-free*; they are one step up from regular languages in Chomsky's hierarchy.

Before giving a precise definition of this class of abstract machines, we will recall the main operations available in stacks. A stack is a sequence of elements (possibly empty) where elements can be added on the top and also be taken out from the top. Stacks are often associated with the acronym "LIFO", which stands for "last in, first out", referring to the fact that new elements are pushed onto the top, and elements are read and removed also from the top.

A push-down automaton can read the top element of the stack (and only the top element) and can put a new element at the top of the stack. The latter operation is called *push*. It is also possible to remove the top element of the stack. This operation is called *pop*. The elements in the stack, as well as the input symbols for the push-down automaton, must belong to a given alphabet. It is usually assumed that a push-down automaton can use different alphabets for the input and the stack.

The operational behaviour of a push-down automaton can be described similarly to a non-deterministic finite automaton, but there is a crucial difference: The transition function is now governed by the input symbol and the symbol in the top of the stack. The push-down automaton starts on a distinguished (initial) state with an empty stack. It reads an input symbol and the symbol from the top of the stack (if the stack is not empty), and according to this pair of values, a transition to a new state (or set of states) is defined. We will assume that each time a symbol is read from the stack, it is removed.

Thus, the current state, the input symbol, and the symbol at the top of the stack determine a set of states to which the machine can move. If, at the end of the input, the machine is in a final state (also called an accepting state), then the word containing the sequence of input symbols read is recognised.

Actually, it is possible to define transitions that ignore the input symbol or the value in the top of the stack. These are called ϵ-transitions (recall that ϵ represents the empty string) because we can always assume that there is an empty string in front of the first input symbol or on top of the element on the top of the stack.

We are now ready to define PDA formally.

Definition 2.12 (Push-down automaton)

A push-down automaton is a tuple $(\mathcal{X}, Q, \Gamma, q_0, F, \delta)$ where

1. $\mathcal{X}$ is an alphabet;

2. Q is a finite set of states $\{q_0, \ldots, q_n\}$;

3. Γ is the alphabet of the stack;

4. $q_0 \in Q$ is the initial state;

5. $F \subseteq Q$ is the subset of final states; and

6. δ is the transition function from tuples containing a state, an input symbol (or ϵ), and a stack symbol (or ϵ) to sets of pairs made up of a state and stack:
$$\delta : Q \times (\mathcal{X} \cup \epsilon) \times (\Gamma \cup \epsilon) \to \mathcal{P}(Q \times (\Gamma \cup \epsilon))$$

Note that Γ was not part of the definition of finite automata (see Definition 2.3). The transition function δ for a given state is now defined on pairs (input, stack-top) and produces as a result a set of pairs (state, stack-top). Indeed, non-determinism is built into the definition (because δ returns a set and because of the existence of ϵ-transitions). If we restrict ourselves to deterministic PDAs, we obtain machines that have strictly less power. In this sense, the properties of PDAs are different from the properties of finite automata since for finite automata the non-determinism of δ does not add any power; deterministic and non-deterministic finite automata recognise the same class of languages.

We can depict a push-down automaton as a machine in the same way as we represented finite automata in Figure 2.1; we just need to add a stack, which the control unit can consult and update.

In the previous section, we described two languages that are not recognisable by finite automata (we used the Pumping Lemma for this):

1. $\{(^n)^n\}$ for any number n (that is, the set of strings containing n opening brackets followed by the same number of closing brackets);

2. $\{w\overline{w} \mid w$ is a string of 0s and 1s and $\overline{w}$ is its mirror image $\}$.

PDAs can recognise these languages because it is possible to use the stack to memorise a string of symbols of any given length. For instance, to recognise the first language, a push-down automaton can push all the '(' symbols in the stack and start popping them when it reads a ')' symbol. Then, the word is accepted if at the end of the input string the stack is empty.

Formally, we define a push-down automaton recognising the language

$$\{(^n)^n \mid n \text{ is a natural number}\}$$

as follows.

Let Q be the set $\{q_1, q_2, q_3, q_4\}$, where q_1 is the initial state. The input alphabet, $\mathcal{X}$, contains the symbols (and). The stack's alphabet, Γ, contains just the symbol (and a marker 0. The final states are q_1 and q_4, and the transition function contains the following moves:

$\delta(q_1, \epsilon, \epsilon)$	$= \{(q_2, 0)\}$	Starting from the initial state, and without reading the input or the stack, the automaton moves to state q_2 and pushes 0 onto the stack.
$\delta(q_2, (, \epsilon)$	$= \{(q_2, ()\}$	If in the state q_2 the input symbol is (, without reading the stack the automaton remains in q_2 and pushes (onto the stack.
$\delta(q_2,), ()$	$= \{(q_3, \epsilon)\}$	If in the state q_2 the input symbol is) and there is a symbol (on top of the stack, the automaton moves to q_3; the symbol (is removed from the stack.
$\delta(q_3,), ()$	$= \{(q_3, \epsilon)\}$	If in the state q_3 the input symbol is) and there is a (on top of the stack, then the automaton remains in q_3; the symbol (is removed from the stack.
$\delta(q_3, \epsilon, 0)$	$= \{(q_4, \epsilon)\}$	If in the state q_3 the top of the stack is 0, then the automaton moves to q_4, which is a final state.

As usual, the automaton starts in the initial state with an empty stack, but in this case the first transition will put a mark 0 in the stack and move to a state q_2 in which all the open brackets in the input word will be pushed onto the stack. The presence of a closing bracket in the input word will trigger a transition to state q_3, and an open bracket is popped from the stack. Then, the automaton remains in state q_3 while there are closing brackets in the input word and open brackets in the stack. If the word belongs to the language, the input word will finish at the same time as we reach the 0 in the stack. However, if the input word contains fewer closing brackets, then the automaton will be blocked in q_3, which is not an accepting state. Similarly, if the input word contains more closing brackets than open brackets, the automaton will be blocked in q_4.

Note that the word is recognised only if the automaton has reached a final state at the end of the input. While there are symbols in the input word, even if the automaton reaches a final state, the computation is not finished (the automaton remains blocked if no transitions are defined).

Finite automata and PDAs are useful tools for the implementation of compilers and interpreters (typically, lexical analysers are specified as finite automata and parsers are defined using PDAs). Although PDAs are strictly more powerful than finite automata, their power is limited. In the previous section, we used the Pumping Lemma to characterise the class of regular languages. It is possible to prove a Pumping Lemma for context-free languages, but the characterisation is more involved: Words in context-free languages can be divided into five parts, such that the second and fourth parts can be repeated together any number of times and the result is still a word in the same language.

We will not state the Pumping Lemma for PDAs here; instead we finish this section with an example of a language that can be shown to be outside the class of context-free languages: $\{a^n b^n c^n \mid n \geq 0\}$.

2.4 Turing machines

A Turing machine is a universal model of computation in the sense that all computable functions can be defined using a Turing machine. We can see a Turing machine as an automaton, a generalisation of a push-down automaton where we have an unlimited amount of memory and no restriction on the positions that can be read from this memory (it is no longer a stack).

We can also think of a Turing machine as a specification of a formal language: The languages that can be recognised by Turing machines form the topmost category in Chomsky's hierarchy. However, it is not possible to decide, in general, whether or not a word belongs to the language associated with a Turing machine. This is a consequence of the undecidability of the Halting problem: It is not possible to decide, given a Turing machine and an input word, whether the machine will halt in an accepting state or not.

The memory of a Turing machine is usually represented by an infinite tape with a head that can read and write symbols and move in both directions on the tape. In this way, the machine can store information on the tape and later move back to read it. The other important component of the machine is its control unit, represented by a set of states and a transition function that governs the changes of state.

Similarly to the other automata discussed in this section, a Turing machine has a distinguished state called the *initial state*. The machine always starts from the initial state and with a tape containing only the input string (that is, the tape is blank everywhere else). We also assume that the head is positioned on the first symbol of the input string when the machine starts.

The machine will make transitions depending on the symbol that the head reads, and it can write on the tape and move the head one position to the left or to the right (this will be indicated by the letters L and R). It continues until a final state is reached. If we think of the machine as recognising a certain language, then it is useful to include two final states q_{reject} and q_{accept}. If an input word belongs to the language, the machine will halt in the final state "accept" (q_{accept}); otherwise it will halt in the final state "reject" (q_{reject}) or it could continue forever, never halting (recall the undecidability results for languages associated with Turing machines discussed in Chapter 1).

At each point during the computation, the situation of the machine can be described by giving the state in which the control is, the contents of the tape, and the position of the head on the tape. These three data define the machine's *configuration*. So the computation of a Turing machine can be described as a sequence of configurations. The transition function indicates how to pass from one configuration to the next one. This sequence of configurations can of course be infinite. If it is finite, the state in the last configuration must be a final state.

Before giving the formal definition of a Turing machine, let us see an example of a language that can be recognised with a Turing machine.

Example 2.13

Consider natural numbers written in unary notation; that is, each number is represented by a string of 1s. The number 0 is represented by the empty string, and any positive number n is represented by a sequence containing n occurrences of the symbol 1. For instance, the number 3 is represented by the string 111. The language

$$\{1^{2^n} \mid n \geq 0\}$$

(that is, the language of the strings that represent a power of 2 in unary notation) can be recognised using a Turing machine. The informal description of the machine is as follows.

Assume we start the machine with a number in unary notation written on the tape (surrounded by blanks) and the reading head on the leftmost position in this number.

1. If the head is on blank when we start, reject.

2. Otherwise, starting on the first 1, move to the end of the string (i.e., the first blank symbol), changing every other 1 into •.

   a) If the tape contained just one 1, accept.

   b) If the number of 1s was odd, reject.

3. Return the head to the beginning of the input.

4. Repeat.

The idea is that each iteration changes half of the 1s into •. If the number is a power of 2 in unary notation (that is, if the string contains a number of 1s that is a power of 2), we will eventually end up with just one 1 and accept the input.

We have given above a description of an algorithm to check whether the length of a string of 1s is a power of 2. Below we specify this algorithm formally, but first we will formally define a Turing machine.

Definition 2.14 (Turing machine)

A Turing machine is a tuple $(Q, \mathcal{X}, \Gamma, \delta, q_0, F)$ where

1. Q is a finite set of states;

2. $\mathcal{X}$ is the input alphabet, which cannot contain the blank symbol;

3. Γ is the tape alphabet, containing the input alphabet and the blank symbol;

4. δ is the transition function,

$$\delta : Q \times \Gamma \to Q \times \Gamma \times \{L, R\}$$

5. $q_0 \in Q$ is a distinguished state, called the *initial state*; and

6. $F \subseteq Q$ is the set of final states, and we assume that it contains two distinguished states, q_{reject} and q_{accept}.

When the machine is started, the tape contains an input string surrounded by blanks, the head is in the first symbol of the input string, and the machine is in the state q_0. As the computation proceeds, the situation of the machine, or *configuration*, is described by a triple containing the current state, the contents of the tape, and the position of the head on the tape.

If the machine reaches the state q_{accept}, it stops. We say that the machine has *accepted* the input. If it reaches the state q_{reject}, it also stops, and we say that the machine has rejected the input. The machine can also loop forever.

Definition 2.15

A language L over the alphabet $\mathcal{X}$ is *recognised* by a Turing machine M if the machine accepts every word in L and rejects every word over $\mathcal{X}$ that is not in L. We will say that a language L is *decidable* if there is a Turing machine that recognises L.

Example 2.16

We now give a formal description of the Turing machine that recognises the language

$$\{1^{2^n} \mid n \geq 0\}$$

Let Q be the set of states $\{q_1, q_2, q_3, q_4, q_5, q_{reject}, q_{accept}\}$, where q_1 is the initial state and q_{reject}, q_{accept} are the final states. The input alphabet, $\mathcal{X}$, contains only the symbol 1. The tape alphabet, Γ, also contains 1 and additionally the blank symbol $\circ$ and a marker $\bullet$. We give the transition function using a diagram in Figure 2.3. In the diagram, states are represented as nodes in a graph and transitions are represented by directed edges (arrows). Each arrow is labelled by the symbol read, the symbol written, and the direction in which the head moves. For instance, the arrow from q_1 to q_2 labelled by $1 \circ R$ indicates that $\delta(q_1, 1) = (q_2, \circ, R)$. In other words, there is a transition from q_1 to q_2 when the symbol read is 1; the machine writes $\circ$ and moves to the right. The arrow pointing to q_1 indicates that this is the initial state.

In this example, we have used the machine as a device to recognise the words of the language; however, a Turing machine can also be seen as a device to perform computations. In this case, the Turing machine represents an algorithm that receives an input and computes an *output* that is written on the tape. For instance, we can use a Turing machine to compute arithmetic functions (addition, multiplication, etc.), as the following example shows.

Example 2.17

We describe informally a Turing machine that computes the double of a number (its input) written in binary notation on the tape. The machine has an initial state q_0 and an accepting state q_{accept} (q_{reject} is not used in this example). The input alphabet is $\{0, 1\}$, and the tape alphabet is the same, with the addition

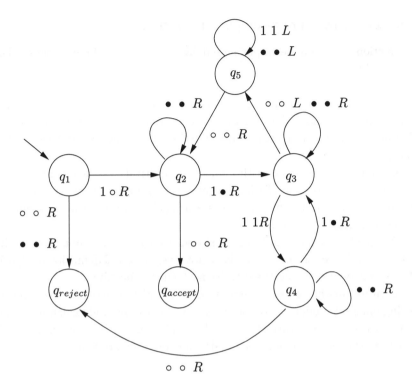

Figure 2.3 Transition function

of a blank symbol. The machine starts in the initial state, q_0, with the head on top of the first binary digit. While there are digits in the input word (either 0 or 1), the machine moves to the right and remains in q_0. Finally, when arriving at a blank symbol, the machine replaces it by 0 and moves to the final state q_{accept}.

We will say that a Turing machine *implements* a partial function f from I to O, where I and O are sets of words (I is the set of possible inputs and O the set of outputs) if whenever the machine starts from a word w in I, with the head in the first symbol of w, the machine halts in the final state q_{accept} and leaves the word $f(w)$ on the tape when f is defined in w. If $f(w)$ is not defined, then the machine may never halt. Thus, if the function f is total (that is, it is defined for all its possible inputs) and there is a Turing machine that implements it, we can see the Turing machine as an algorithm to compute the function (recall that an algorithm must always produce a result).

Definition 2.18 (Turing-computable functions)

A function that can be implemented by a Turing machine is called Turing computable.

Thus, if a function is Turing computable, a Turing machine that implements it is a representation of an algorithm to compute the function. The question that arises is whether all computable functions can be defined in terms of Turing machines.

Church's Thesis answers this question positively. It says that, given any algorithm, there is some Turing machine that implements it. In other words, if a function is computable, then it is Turing computable (that is, computable by some Turing machine).

Although this thesis is formally stated, we cannot attempt to prove it because it is not precise enough; we have not given a formal definition of algorithm that is independent from the definition of Turing machine.

It turns out that all other definitions of algorithm that have been proposed (using different models of computation, such as the Lambda calculus, recursive functions, etc.) have turned out to be equivalent to Turing machines. This provides evidence for Church's Thesis (but does not prove it).

2.4.1 Variants of Turing machines

The definition of a Turing machine that we have given is one of many available in the literature. Some definitions involve more elements than the one we gave or impose more restrictions than we did.

For instance, there are non-deterministic Turing machines, which take their name from the fact that the transition function is non-deterministic. In a non-deterministic Turing machine, given a configuration, there are several possible moves, so the next configuration is not uniquely determined.

Similarly to finite automata (and unlike PDAs), non-deterministic Turing machines have the same computation power as deterministic ones in the sense that they recognise the same languages or compute the same functions.

Other variants of Turing machines use several infinite tapes instead of only one tape, and again it is possible to show that these machines are equivalent in power to the machines with only one tape.

Still another variant uses one tape but limited in one direction: The tape has a starting point but has no bound to the right, so the machine can move an infinite number of steps towards the right. It is possible also to limit the alphabet, for instance by reducing the tape alphabet to just two symbols. Again, these variants have exactly the same power.

2.4.2 The universal Turing machine

It is possible to give a code for each Turing machine, so that from the code we can retrieve the machine. An easy way of doing this is as follows.

Assume the machine has n states $q_0, \ldots, q_{n-1}$, where each q_i is a number, q_0 is the initial state, and the last m states are final. Also assume that the input alphabet is $\{1\}$ and the tape alphabet is $\{0, 1\}$ (where 0 plays the role of a blank symbol). It is well known that a binary alphabet is sufficient to encode any kind of data, so there is no loss of generality in making this assumption. The transition function can be represented as a table, or equivalently a list of 5-tuples of the form (q, s, q', s', d), where q represents the current state, s the symbol on the tape under the head, q' the new state, s' the symbol written on the tape, and d the direction of movement, which we will write as $0, 1$. The order of the tuples is not important here. Thus, we can assume without loss of generality that the transition function is represented by a list l of tuples. The full description of the machine under these assumptions is given by the tuple (n, m, l), where l is the list representing the transition function, n the number of states, and m the number of final states, as indicated above. We will say that the tuple is the *code* for the machine since from it we can recover the original machine. In fact, the code for the machine is not unique since we can reorder the list l and still obtain an equivalent machine.

Now we can see the codes of Turing machines as words, and as such they can be used as input for a Turing machine. It is then possible to define a Turing machine U such that, when the code of a machine A is written on the tape, together with an input word w for A, U decodes it and simulates the behaviour of the machine A on w. The machine U is usually called the *universal Turing machine*.

2.5 Imperative programming

The work done by Turing on abstract computation models had a deep influence on the design of computers and later on the design of programming languages for those computers. The main components of Turing abstract machines are present in the von Neumann architecture of modern computers: a memory, which can be thought of as infinite if we consider not only the RAM but also the storage available through disks and other peripherals; and a control unit that governs the work of the machine. We can see modern computers as implementations of Turing's universal machine. The memory is one of the main components of the computer, storing instructions and data, and the other important component is the processor.

The first programming languages were designed to follow closely the physical design of the machine. The languages that evolved from them, usually called *imperative* programming languages, are still influenced by the architecture of the computer. Imperative languages are abstractions of the underlying von Neumann machine in the sense that they retain the essential parts but drop out complicating, superfluous details. Low-level languages provide a very limited level of abstraction, whereas a high-level language can be seen as a virtual machine where, in general, memory manipulation is transparent for the programmer and input/output primitives are hardware independent.

Although the level of abstraction provided by imperative languages varies greatly from assembly languages to sophisticated languages such as Java, there are common features in the design of all the imperative languages that reflect the underlying machine architecture. The memory and processor, the main components of the machine, are abstracted in a high-level imperative language by variables, representing memory space, together with assignment instructions that modify their contents, and control structures that indicate the order of execution of instructions in the processor.

The influence of Turing's work is not limited to computer architecture and the design of the first imperative programming languages. Abstract machines based on the notion of a state transition are used nowadays to give a precise meaning to language constructs in use in imperative languages. Indeed, the first approach to giving a precise, formal description of the behaviour of programming language constructs was in terms of an abstract machine, or more precisely a transition system specifying an interpreter for the programming language.

2.6 Further reading

For more information on automata theory, we refer the interested reader to [47, 24]. Further information on Church's Thesis and ways to prove it can be found in the recent article [12]. For more information on the use of abstract machines as a tool to describe the semantics of imperative programming languages, we refer to [15, 37, 53].

2.7 Exercises

1. Consider the alphabet $\{0, 1\}$. Describe (graphically or formally)

   a) a finite automaton that recognises the language of the strings of 0s of any length;

   b) a finite automaton that recognises the language of the strings of 0s and 1s that contain a 1 in the second position;

   c) a finite automaton that recognises the language of the strings of 0s and 1s that start and finish with 00 and do not contain 11.

2. Build finite automata with alphabet $\{0, 1\}$ to recognise

   a) the language of strings that have three consecutive 0s;

   b) the language of strings that do not have three consecutive 1s.

3. Describe a finite automaton that recognises words over the alphabet $\{a, b, c\}$ with an odd number of symbols and such that they do not contain aa or bb.

4. Let A be a finite automaton. Show that the set of subwords (that is, pre-fixes, suffixes, or any continuous segment) of the words in the language $L(A)$ can also be recognised by a finite automaton.

5. Use the Pumping Lemma to show that the language L containing all the words of the form $a^n b^n c^n$, for any $n \geq 0$, cannot be recognised by a finite automaton.

6. How can a push-down automaton recognise the language

   $$\{w\overline{w} \mid w \text{ is a string of 0s and 1s and } \overline{w} \text{ is its mirror image}\}?$$

   Give an informal description of such an automaton.

7. Show that the class of languages recognisable by push-down automata (i.e., the class of context-free languages) is closed under union and concatenation but not under intersection.

8. Describe a Turing machine that recognises the language of the strings $w \bullet w$, where w is a string over an alphabet $\{0, 1\}$.

9. Define a Turing machine that, for any word w over the alphabet $\{0, 1\}$, outputs ww (that is, the machine starts with w and halts with a tape containing ww).

10. Show that if a language L over the alphabet $\mathcal{X}$ can be recognised by a Turing machine, then the following languages are also recognisable:

a) the complement of L (that is, the set of all the strings over $\mathcal{X}$ that are not in L);

b) the union of L and another decidable language L';

c) the concatenation of L and another decidable language L' (that is, the language consisting of all the words that can be formed by concatenating a word from L and a word from L');

d) the intersection of L and another decidable language L'.

11. Define a Turing machine that accepts the words from the alphabet $\{a, b, c\}$ such that the number of occurrences of each character in the word is exactly the same.

3
The Lambda Calculus

The Lambda calculus, or λ-calculus, is a model of computation based on the idea that algorithms can be seen as mathematical functions mapping inputs to outputs. It was introduced by Alonzo Church in the 1930s as a precise notation for a theory of anonymous functions; its name is due to the use of the Greek letter λ in functional expressions. Church remarked that when denoting a function by an expression such as $x + y$, it was not always clear what the intended function was. For instance, the expression $x + y$ can be interpreted as

1. the number $x + y$, where x and y are some given numbers;

2. the function $f : x \mapsto x + y$ that associates to a number x the number $x + y$ for some predetermined value y;

3. the function $g : y \mapsto x + y$ that associates to an input y the number $x + y$ for some predetermined value x; or

4. the function $h : x, y \mapsto x + y$, which takes as arguments x and y and outputs the value $x + y$.

This can be a source of ambiguity, and Church proposed a new notation for functions that emphasises the distinction between variables used as arguments and variables that stand for predefined values. In this notation, a function with an argument x is preceded by the symbol λ and the variable x. For instance, the function $f : x \mapsto x + y$ that associates to an input x the number $x + y$ for some predetermined value y is written $\lambda x.x + y$. In particular, the functions mentioned above can be easily distinguished using the λ-calculus notation:

– The number $x + y$ is written just $x + y$.

– The function $f : x \mapsto x + y$ is written $\lambda x.x + y$.

– The function $g : y \mapsto x + y$ is written $\lambda y.x + y$.

– The function $h : x, y \mapsto x + y$ is written $\lambda xy.x + y$.

The λ-calculus is a Turing-complete model of computation. It has exactly the same computational power as Turing machines. Church's work, like Turing's, was motivated by the need to formalise the notion of an algorithm in order to solve some of Hilbert's open problems from the 1900 Congress of Mathematicians. In addition to being a useful tool to analyse computability problems, in recent years the λ-calculus has also been extremely useful to

– give a semantics to programming languages,

– study strategies and implementation techniques for functional languages,

– encode proofs in a variety of logic systems, and

– design automatic theorem provers and proof assistants.

In the rest of this chapter, we will describe the λ-calculus as an abstract model of computation and also as the foundation for the functional programming paradigm. We first give the syntax of terms in the λ-calculus and then associate computations with terms.

3.1 λ-calculus: Syntax

We assume that there is an infinite, countable set of variables x, y, z, $\ldots$, which we will use to define by induction the set of λ-calculus terms (sometimes called λ-terms, or simply terms if there is no ambiguity). There are three kinds of terms in the λ-calculus: *variables*, *abstractions*, and *applications*. Below we give the precise definition.

Definition 3.1 (λ-terms)

The set Λ of λ-terms is the smallest set such that:

– All the variables $x, y, z, \ldots$ are in Λ (that is, variables are λ-terms).

– If x is a variable and M is a λ-term, then $(\lambda x.M)$ is also a λ-term. Such λ-terms are called abstractions.

– If M and N are λ-terms, then $(M\,N)$, called an application, is also a λ-term.

An abstraction $(\lambda x.M)$ can be seen as a function, where x is the *argument* and M is the *function body*. We apply a function to a concrete argument by juxtaposing the function and its argument; if M is a function and N its argument, then the pair $(M\ N)$ represents the application of M to N.

It is traditional to use some conventions to simplify the syntax, avoiding writing too many brackets. In particular:

- We will omit the outermost brackets in abstractions and applications when there is no ambiguity.

- Application associates to the *left*, so instead of writing $((MN)P)$ we will simply write $M\,N\,P$ (by default, if there are no brackets, the left association determines the order of application).

- Abstraction associates to the *right*, so instead of writing $\lambda x.(\lambda y.M)$ we simply write $\lambda x.\lambda y.M$, or even shorter, $\lambda xy.M$.

- We will assume the scope of a λ is as "big" as possible. In order to shorten it, we will use brackets. For example, we write $\lambda x.y\ x$ instead of $\lambda x.(y\ x)$, and we write $(\lambda x.y)\ x$ to limit the scope.

Example 3.2

The following are examples of λ-terms:

- x.

- $\lambda x.x$ — This term represents a function that takes an argument x and returns just x. It is the *identity* function.

- $\lambda x.\lambda y.x$ — This term represents a function that takes two arguments, x and y, and returns the first one.

- $\lambda x.\lambda y.y$ — This term also represents a function with two arguments, but the result is the second one.

- $\lambda x.\lambda y.xy$ — Here the function has two arguments, and the result is obtained by applying the first one to the second one. Although we have not mentioned types yet, it is clear that this term will make sense if the first argument is itself a function.

- $\lambda x.xx$ — This term is usually called *self-application*. It denotes a function that takes an argument x and applies it to itself.

- $\lambda x.y$ — Here we have a function that takes an argument x but does not use it at all. The result of the function is y.

– $\lambda x.yx$ — In this case, x is used as an argument for the function y (a parameter in this expression).

– $\lambda xyz.xz(yz)$ — This is an interesting term that takes three arguments. The first is applied to the third and to the result of the second applied to the third. Here it is important to put the brackets in the expression (yz); otherwise, according to the conventions, we would apply x to three arguments, z, y, z, instead of two.

In a λ-term, it is important to distinguish between variables that are associated with a λ in an abstraction and variables that do not have a corresponding λ. More precisely, in a λ-abstraction $\lambda x.M$, the variable x is *bound* inside M. The variables that are not bound by a λ are said to be *free*. For example, in the term $\lambda x.yx$, the variable x is bound, whereas y is free.

In fact, to be precise, we should talk about free and bound *occurrences* of variables since the same variable may occur many times in a term and some of the occurrences may be bound while others are free. For instance, in the λ-term $x(\lambda x.x)$, the leftmost occurrence of x is free, but since we have on the right a λ-abstraction for x, the occurrence of x in the body of the abstraction is bound. Thus, each occurrence of a variable in a λ-term may be free or bound, depending on whether it is under the scope of a corresponding λ or not.

The set of free variables of a λ-term M will be denoted $FV(M)$. It is defined by induction below.

Definition 3.3 (Free variables)

We define the set of free variables of M, $FV(M)$, as a recursive function. There are three cases, depending on whether M is a variable, an abstraction, or an application:

$$
\begin{aligned}
FV(x) &= \{x\} \\
FV(\lambda x.M) &= FV(M) - \{x\} \\
FV(MN) &= FV(M) \cup FV(N)
\end{aligned}
$$

The definition above is an example of an *inductive definition*: We have defined the set of free variables of a term by induction on the structure of the term. There is a case for each kind of λ-term. In the case of a variable, there is no λ and therefore the variable is free. In an abstraction, the variable attached to the λ is bound in the body, so it is not in the set of free variables. For an application, we compute the set of free variables of the function and the argument and take the union.

Terms without free variables are called *closed terms*. They are also called *combinators*.

Example 3.4

Using the definition above, we can easily see that the term $\lambda z.z$ is closed since the only occurrence of z is bound by the leading λz. In the terms $\lambda x.z$ and $z\lambda x.x$, the variable z occurs free. The term $\lambda xyz.xz(yz)$ is closed since all the variables are bound by a λ.

Similarly, we can define the set of bound variables of a term as follows.

Definition 3.5 (Bound variables)

The function BV computes the set of bound variables of a term:

$$
\begin{aligned}
BV(x) &= \emptyset \\
BV(\lambda x.M) &= \{x\} \cup BV(M) \\
BV(MN) &= BV(M) \cup BV(N)
\end{aligned}
$$

Note that, according to the previous definitions, $FV(x\ (\lambda x.x)) = \{x\}$ and $BV(x\ (\lambda x.x)) = \{x\}$; this is because, as explained above, the first occurrence of x is free but the second is bound by a λ.

In general, if we say that a variable is free in a term, it means that there is at least one free occurrence of this variable.

Since an abstraction $\lambda x.M$ is the representation of a function that uses x as a formal parameter, it is clear that we should obtain an equivalent function if we chose a new variable z, changed x to z, and consistently renamed the occurrences of x in M as z. In other words, the name of a bound variable is not important. We can see the variable just as a placeholder, or a marker that indicates the positions where the argument will be used. Since the name of a bound variable is not important, λ-terms that differ only in the names of their bound variables will be equated. More precisely, we will take the quotient of the set of λ-terms by an equivalence relation, called α-equivalence, that equates terms modulo renaming of variables. The renaming of x by y will be denoted $\{x \mapsto y\}$.

The operation of renaming should be done in a consistent way to preserve the meaning of the term. In particular, we should not *capture* variables during the renaming process. We say that a variable has been captured if it was free before renaming and it becomes bound after renaming. For instance, if we rename x as y in the term $\lambda y.xy$, the occurrence of x becomes y and therefore becomes bound by the leading λ. This is a problem because the meaning of the function has changed. Before renaming, we had a function with argument y that applies some predefined x to y, whereas after renaming we have a function that takes an argument y and applies it to itself. We can solve the problem by first changing y to a different name, for instance z. More precisely,

$$(\lambda y.xy)\{x \mapsto y\} = (\lambda z.xz)\{x \mapsto y\} = (\lambda z.yz)$$

Using renamings, we can now define the α-equivalence relation inductively.

Definition 3.6 (α-equivalence)

The α-equivalence relation on λ-terms, denoted by $=_\alpha$, is generated by the following rules:

- $M =_\alpha N$ if M and N are exactly the same variable: $M = N = x$.
- $M =_\alpha N$ if $M = M_1M_2$, $N = N_1N_2$ and $M_1 =_\alpha N_1$, $M_2 =_\alpha N_2$.
- $M =_\alpha N$ if $M = \lambda x.M_1$, $N = \lambda x.N_1$ and $M_1 =_\alpha N_1$.
- $M =_\alpha N$ if $M = \lambda x.M_1$, $N = \lambda y.N_1$ and there is a fresh variable z such that $M_1\{x \mapsto z\} =_\alpha N_1\{y \mapsto z\}$.

It is an equivalence relation (i.e., it is reflexive, symmetric, and transitive).

The following are concrete examples of α-equalities:

- $\lambda x.x =_\alpha \lambda y.y$.
- $\lambda x.\lambda y.xy =_\alpha \lambda z_1.\lambda z_2.z_1z_2$.
- $(\lambda x.x)z =_\alpha (\lambda y.y)z$.

In what follows, we will consider λ-terms as representatives of equivalence classes for the α-equality relation. More precisely, λ-terms are defined modulo α-equivalence, so $\lambda x.x$ and $\lambda y.y$ are the *same* term. Indeed, we will see that α-equivalent terms have the same computational behaviour.

3.2 Computation

Abstractions represent functions that can be applied to arguments. The main computation rule, called *β-reduction*, indicates how to find the result of a function (i.e., its output) when an argument (i.e., input) is provided.

A *redex* is a term of the form

$$(\lambda x.M)N$$

It represents the application of the function $\lambda x.M$ to the argument N. To obtain the result, the intuitive idea is that we need to perform the operations indicated in the body of the function using the concrete argument N instead of the formal argument x. In other words, inside M (the body of the function $\lambda x.M$) we have to replace the formal argument x by the concrete argument N. This is the main computation rule in the λ-calculus. Formally, we define it as follows.

Definition 3.7 (β-reduction rule)

The reduction scheme

$$(\lambda x.M)N \to_\beta M\{x \mapsto N\}$$

where $(\lambda x.M)N$ is a redex and $M\{x \mapsto N\}$ represents the term obtained when we *substitute* x by N in M is called the β-*reduction rule*.

We write $M \to_\beta M'$ to indicate that M reduces to M' using the β-rule.

We will say that the redex $(\lambda x.M)N$ β-*reduces*, or simply reduces, to the term $M\{x \mapsto N\}$, where $\{x \mapsto N\}$ is a *substitution*. The notion of substitution used here is subtle since we have to take into account the fact that λ-terms are defined modulo α-equivalence. We give the precise definition of substitution below.

The β-reduction rule can be used to reduce a redex anywhere in a λ-term, not necessarily at the top. In other words, we can reduce a subterm inside a λ-term. We say that the rule generates a relation that is closed by context (sometimes this is called a *compatible* relation). Closure by context can be formally defined as follows.

Definition 3.8 (β-reduction relation)

A *context*, denoted $C[-]$, is a λ-term with one free occurrence of a distinguished variable $-$. We write $C[M]$ to denote the term obtained by replacing $-$ with M.

The β-*reduction relation* is a binary relation containing all the pairs $(\lambda x.M)N \to_\beta M\{x \mapsto N\}$ generated by the β-reduction rule and in addition all the pairs $C[M] \to_\beta C[M']$ such that $M \to_\beta M'$.

We write $M \to_\beta M'$ to indicate that the pair of terms M and M' belongs to the β-reduction relation, and we say that M reduces to M' in one step.

It is also useful to have a notation for terms that are related through a chain of zero or more reduction steps. We write $M \to_\beta^* M'$ if there is a sequence of terms $M_1, \ldots, M_n$ (where $n \geq 1$) such that $M = M_1 \to_\beta M_2 \to_\beta \ldots \to_\beta M_n = M'$. Notice that, if $n = 1$, the sequence of reduction steps is empty and M' is M itself. The relation $\to_\beta^*$ is the reflexive and transitive closure of $\to_\beta$.

Before giving the formal definition of substitution, we show some simple examples of reduction.

Example 3.9

– The redex $(\lambda x.x)y$ denotes the application of the identity function to the argument y. The expected result is therefore y. We can see that β-reduction computes exactly that. We have a reduction step $(\lambda x.x)y \rightarrow_\beta x\{x \mapsto y\}$, where $x\{x \mapsto y\}$ represents the term obtained by replacing x by y in x (that is, the term y).

– More interestingly, the term $(\lambda x.\lambda y.x)(\lambda z.z)u$ has a β-redex on the left: $(\lambda x.\lambda y.x)(\lambda z.z)$. This β-redex reduces to the term $\lambda y.\lambda z.z$. Since β-reduction is closed by context, we have a step of reduction $(\lambda x.\lambda y.x)(\lambda z.z)u \rightarrow_\beta (\lambda y.\lambda z.z)u$. The latter still has a β-redex, and can be further reduced to $\lambda z.z$. Thus,

$$(\lambda x\lambda y.x)(\lambda z.z)u \rightarrow_\beta^* \lambda z.z$$

– We also have a reduction sequence:

$$(\lambda x.\lambda y.xy)(\lambda x.x) \rightarrow_\beta \lambda y.(\lambda x.x)y \rightarrow_\beta \lambda y.y$$

Note that we use the word "reduce", but this does not mean that the term on the right is any simpler. For example, if the function is the self-application term $\lambda x.xx$ and we apply it to the last term in Example 3.2, we have a reduction step:

$$(\lambda x.xx)(\lambda xyz.xz(yz)) \rightarrow_\beta (\lambda xyz.xz(yz))(\lambda xyz.xz(yz))$$

3.2.1 Substitution

Substitution in the λ-calculus is a special kind of replacement. $M\{x \mapsto N\}$ means replace all *free* occurrences of x in M by the term N without capturing free variables of N.

The reason why we only replace free occurrences of variables is clear: λ-terms are defined modulo α-equivalence; bound variables stand for unknown arguments of functions.

The definition of substitution also takes into account the fact that in replacing x by N inside a λ-term M we should preserve the meaning of the term N. In particular, if N contains free variables, they should remain free after the replacement has been done. For instance, it would be wrong to replace y in $\lambda z.yz$ by a term containing z free. Indeed, consider the substitution $\{y \mapsto z\}$

and the term $\lambda z.yz$. If we replace without taking into account binders, we obtain $(\lambda z.zz)$ — the self-application. However, since $\lambda z.yz$ is a representative of an equivalence class, we could have taken instead any other representative, for instance $\lambda x.yx$, which is α-equivalent. The replacement in this case would produce $\lambda x.zx$, which is not a self-application. In the first case, we say that the variable z was *captured*; this is something that should be avoided.

To avoid capturing variables, it is sufficient to rename the bound variables appropriately. The operation of renaming boils down to choosing a different representative of an α-equivalence class, which is permitted since λ-terms are defined modulo α-equivalence.

We are now ready to define, by induction, the operation of substitution of a variable x by a term N in M, avoiding capture.

Definition 3.10 (Substitution)

The result of $M\{x \mapsto N\}$ is defined by induction on the structure of M, with cases for variable, application, and abstraction. If M is a variable, there are two subcases, depending on whether M is x or a different variable. The case for abstraction is also divided into subcases:

$$
\begin{aligned}
x\{x \mapsto N\} &= N \\
y\{x \mapsto N\} &= y \\
(PQ)\{x \mapsto N\} &= (P\{x \mapsto N\})(Q\{x \mapsto N\}) \\
(\lambda x.P)\{x \mapsto N\} &= (\lambda x.P) \\
(\lambda y.P)\{x \mapsto N\} &= \lambda y.(P\{x \mapsto N\}) && \text{if } x \notin FV(P) \\
&&& \text{or } y \notin FV(N) \\
(\lambda y.P)\{x \mapsto N\} &= (\lambda z.P\{y \mapsto z\})\{x \mapsto N\} && \text{if } x \in FV(P) \\
&&& \text{and } y \in FV(N), \\
&&& \text{where } z \text{ is fresh}
\end{aligned}
$$

In the last line, we have used a fresh variable z; that is, a variable that does not occur in the expressions under consideration. This is to avoid capturing the variable y that occurs free in the term N.

Example 3.11

Let us apply the definition above to compute $(\lambda z.yz)\{y \mapsto z\}$; in other words, we will compute the result of the substitution $\{y \mapsto z\}$ on the term $\lambda z.yz$. In this case, the term is an abstraction with bound variable z, and y is free in the body of the abstraction. Also, the substitution will replace y by a term that contains z free (the term to be substituted for y is precisely z). Therefore, we are in the last case of the definition above, and before replacing y we need to rename the bound variable. Since x does not occur in any of the expressions in our example, we can choose x as a fresh variable. Thus

$$(\lambda z.yz)\{y \mapsto z\} = (\lambda x.(yz)\{z \mapsto x\})\{y \mapsto z\}$$

According to the definition above,

$$(yz)\{z \mapsto x\} = (y\{z \mapsto x\})(z\{z \mapsto x\}) = (yx)$$

Using this equality, we obtain

$$(\lambda z.yz)\{y \mapsto z\} = (\lambda x.yx)\{y \mapsto z\}$$

and now we can apply the second case for abstraction in Definition 3.10 together with the cases for application and variables, obtaining

$$(\lambda z.yz)\{y \mapsto z\} = (\lambda x.zx)$$

A useful property of substitution is the following, known as the Substitution Lemma.

Property 3.12

If $x \notin FV(P)$, $(M\{x \mapsto N\})\{y \mapsto P\} = (M\{y \mapsto P\})\{x \mapsto N\{y \mapsto P\}\}$.

3.2.2 Normal forms

Computation in the λ-calculus is a *reduction* process using the β-rule. A natural question arises: When do we stop reducing? In other words, if computation is reduction, we need to know when we have found the result.

There are several notions of "result" in the λ-calculus; we define two below.

– *Normal form:* A simple answer to the question above is: Stop reducing when there are no redexes left to reduce.

A *normal form* is a term that does not contain any redexes.

A term that can be reduced to a term in normal form is said to be *normalisable*. Formally, M is normalisable if there exists a normal form N such that $M \to_\beta^* N$. For example,

$$\lambda abc.((\lambda x.a(\lambda y.xy))b\ c) \to_\beta \lambda abc.(a(\lambda y.by)c)$$

and the latter is a normal form (recall that application associates to the left).

– *Weak head normal form:* Another notion of result that is very useful in functional programming requires reducing the β-redexes that are not under an abstraction. In other words, we stop reducing when there are no redexes left but without reducing under an abstraction. For example,

$$\lambda abc.((\lambda x.a(\lambda y.xy))b\ c)$$

is a weak head normal form but not a normal form.

3.2.3 Properties of reductions

Since we can view a λ-term as a program and normal forms as a notion of result, it is important to study the properties of the reduction relation that will allow us to obtain the result associated with a program. The first question here is whether, given a program, there is a result at all. If there is a result, we may wonder whether that result is unique. Indeed, each term has at most one normal form in the λ-calculus, and some terms have none.

Some of the most interesting properties of reduction relations are stated below.

– *Confluence:* A reduction relation is confluent if peaks of reductions (i.e., two reduction sequences branching out of the same term) are always joinable. More precisely, $\rightarrow$ is confluent if, whenever $M \rightarrow^* M_1$ and $M \rightarrow^* M_2$, there exists a term M_3 such that $M_1 \rightarrow^* M_3$ and $M_2 \rightarrow^* M_3$.

The β-reduction relation in the λ-calculus is confluent.

– *Normalisation:* A term is normalisable if there exists a sequence of reductions that ends in a normal form.

Some λ-terms are not β-normalisable.

– *Strong Normalisation (or Termination):* A term M is strongly normalisable, or terminating, if all reduction sequences starting from M are finite.

The λ-calculus is confluent but not strongly normalising (or even normalising), as witnessed by the term $(\lambda x.xx)(\lambda x.xx)$; this term is usually called Ω.

Each λ-term has at most one normal form: this *unicity of normal forms* is a consequence of the confluence property of β-reduction (the proof of this result is left as an exercise; see Section 3.8).

3.2.4 Reduction strategies

If a term has a normal form, there may be many different reduction sequences leading to that normal form (and the same can happen if we try to reduce to a weak head normal form). For instance, we can build the following kinds of reduction sequences:

— *Leftmost-outermost reduction:* If a term has several redexes, we first reduce the one at the leftmost-outermost position in the term; that is, the first redex starting from the left that is not contained in any other redex.

— *Leftmost-innermost reduction:* If a term has several redexes, we first reduce the one at the leftmost-innermost position in the term; that is, the first redex, starting from the left, that does not have any other redex inside.

A function that, given a term, selects a position to reduce is called a *strategy*. Leftmost-outermost and leftmost-innermost are two examples of strategies. The choice of strategy can make a huge difference in how many reduction steps are needed and on whether we may find a normal form at all (when one exists).

The leftmost-outermost strategy always finds the normal form of the term if there is one. For this reason, it is usually called a *normalising strategy*. However, it may be inefficient (in the sense that there may be other strategies that find the normal form in fewer reduction steps). We show a simple example below.

Example 3.13

Consider the term $\lambda x.xxx$ and assume we apply it to the term $(\lambda y.y)z$. We give two reduction sequences below; the first one follows the leftmost-outermost strategy, whereas the second one is a leftmost-innermost reduction.

Leftmost-outermost reduction:

$$
\begin{aligned}
(\lambda x.xxx)((\lambda y.y)z) \quad &\rightarrow_\beta \quad ((\lambda y.y)z)((\lambda y.y)z)((\lambda y.y)z) \\
&\rightarrow_\beta \quad z((\lambda y.y)z)((\lambda y.y)z) \\
&\rightarrow_\beta \quad zz((\lambda y.y)z) \\
&\rightarrow_\beta \quad zzz
\end{aligned}
$$

Leftmost-innermost reduction:

$$
\begin{aligned}
(\lambda x.xxx)((\lambda y.y)z) \quad &\rightarrow_\beta \quad (\lambda x.xxx)z \\
&\rightarrow_\beta \quad zzz
\end{aligned}
$$

Most functional programming languages reduce terms (more precisely, programs) to weak head normal form (i.e., they do not reduce under abstractions). This is because if the normal form of a program is an abstraction, that means the result is a function; reduction does not proceed until some arguments are provided.

Although reduction to weak head normal form is standard in functional languages, there is no consensus as to which is the best strategy of reduction to implement. Several choices are possible:

1. *Call-by-name* (also called *normal order of reduction*): Arguments are evaluated each time they are needed. This corresponds to an outermost reduction.

2. *Call-by-value* (also called *applicative order of reduction*). Arguments are evaluated first and the reduced terms are then used in the substitution (avoiding duplication of work). This corresponds to an innermost reduction.

3. *Lazy evaluation*: Arguments are evaluated only if needed, and at most once. Lazy evaluation is similar to call-by-name in that arguments are evaluated when they are needed, but it imposes a further restriction in that they are only evaluated once to improve efficiency.

Most functional languages implement either a call-by-value or a lazy evaluation strategy.

3.3 Arithmetic functions

The syntax of the λ-calculus is very simple: Terms can be variables, applications, or λ-abstractions. We have not given any syntax to represent numbers or data structures. It turns out that no additional syntax is necessary for this. It is possible to represent numbers, and general data structures, in the λ-calculus, as we will see below.

Definition 3.14 (Church numerals)

We can define the natural numbers as follows:

$$
\begin{aligned}
\overline{0} &= \lambda x.\lambda y.y \\
\overline{1} &= \lambda x.\lambda y.x \; y \\
\overline{2} &= \lambda x.\lambda y.x(x \; y) \\
\overline{3} &= \lambda x.\lambda y.x(x(x \; y)) \\
&\;\;\vdots
\end{aligned}
$$

These are called *Church integers* or *Church numerals*. Below we write $\overline{n}$ to denote the Church numeral representing the number n.

Using this representation of numbers, we can define the arithmetic functions. For example, the successor function that takes $\overline{n}$ and returns $\overline{n+1}$ is defined by the λ-term

$$S = \lambda x.\lambda y.\lambda z.y(x\ y\ z)$$

To check it, we see that when we apply this function to the representation of the number n, we obtain the representation of the number $n + 1$:

$$
\begin{aligned}
S\overline{n} &= (\lambda x.\lambda y.\lambda z.y((x\ y)z))(\lambda x.\lambda y.x \ldots (x(x\ y))) \\
&\to_\beta \lambda y.\lambda z.y((\lambda x.\lambda y.x \ldots (x(x\ y))\ y)z) \\
&\to_\beta^* \lambda y.\lambda z.y(y \ldots (y(y\ z)) = \overline{n+1}
\end{aligned}
$$

In the rest of the chapter, we will often call the Church numerals simply "numbers". In general, to define an arithmetic function f that requires k arguments

$$f : Nat^k \mapsto Nat$$

we will use a λ-term $\lambda x_1 \ldots x_k.M$, which will be applied to k numbers: $(\lambda x_1 \ldots x_k.M)\overline{n_1} \ldots \overline{n_k}$.

For example, the following term defines addition:

$$ADD = \lambda x.\lambda y.\lambda a.\lambda b.(x\ a)(y\ a\ b)$$

We can check that this term indeed behaves like the addition function by applying it to two arbitrary Church numerals $\overline{m}$ and $\overline{n}$ and computing the result (which will be $\overline{m+n}$). We leave this as an exercise; see Section 3.8.

3.4 Booleans

We can also represent the Boolean values True and False, as well as the Boolean functions, using just variables, abstraction, and application.

Definition 3.15 (Booleans)

We define the constants *True* and *False* by the following terms:

$$
\begin{aligned}
False &= \lambda x.\lambda y.y \\
True &= \lambda x.\lambda y.x
\end{aligned}
$$

Using these representations, we can now define Boolean functions such as *NOT*, *AND*, *OR*, etc. For example, the function NOT is defined by the λ-term

$$NOT = \lambda x.x\ False\ True$$

We can check that this definition is correct by applying it to the representation of the Boolean constants:

$$NOT\ False = (\lambda x.x\ False\ True)False \rightarrow_\beta False\ False\ True \rightarrow_\beta True$$

and

$$NOT\ True = (\lambda x.x\ False\ True)True \rightarrow_\beta True\ False\ True \rightarrow_\beta False$$

Using the same ideas, we can define a λ-term that behaves like a conditional construct in a programming language. We will call it *IF*, and it is the λ-calculus implementation of an if-then-else statement:

$$IF = \lambda x.\lambda y.\lambda z.x\ y\ z$$

It is easy to see that

$$IF\ B\ E_1\ E_2 \rightarrow_\beta^* E_1 \qquad \text{if } B = True$$

and

$$IF\ B\ E_1\ E_2 \rightarrow_\beta^* E_2 \qquad \text{if } B = False$$

Instead of *IF B E_1 E_2*, we may write *IF B THEN E_1 ELSE E_2*.

Example 3.16

The function *is-zero?* can be defined as

$$\lambda n.n(True\ False)True$$

Then

$$is\text{-}zero?\ \overline{0} \rightarrow_\beta^* True$$

and

$$is\text{-}zero?\ \overline{n} \rightarrow_\beta^* False \quad \text{if } n > 0.$$

We can use *IF* and *is-zero?* to define the *SIGN* function:

$$SIGN = \lambda n.IF\ (is\text{-}zero?\ n)\ THEN\ \overline{0}\ ELSE\ \overline{1}$$

3.5 Recursion

Assume we know how to compute multiplication, the predecessor, and a test for zero, and we want to define the familiar factorial function on natural numbers (that is, a function that associates with 0 the value 1 and for any number $n > 0$ it evaluates to the product of n and the factorial of $n - 1$). Our goal will be to define a λ-term $FACT$ that when applied to a number produces as a result the factorial of this number. In other words, the normal form of $FACT\,\overline{n}$ should be the number representing the factorial of n.

As a first attempt, we can write

$$FACT \;=\; \lambda n.IF\,(\textit{is-zero? }n) \quad THEN\;\overline{1}$$
$$ELSE\;(MULT\,n\,(FACT\,(PRED\,n)))$$

However, this is not a well-defined λ-term since we are using inside the definition of $FACT$ the term $FACT$ that we are trying to define!

There is a solution to this problem via the so-called *fix point* operators of the λ-calculus. A fix point operator is a λ-term that computes fix points, or in other words a λ-term Y such that for any term M

$$Y\;M =_\beta M(Y\;M)$$

where $=_\beta$ is the reflexive, symmetric, and transitive closure of $\rightarrow_\beta$. In this case, we say that Y computes the fix point of M.

For instance, we can take

$$Y = \lambda h.(\lambda x.h(x\;x))(\lambda x.h(x\;x))$$

or even better

$$Y_T = AA \quad \text{where} \quad A = \lambda a.\lambda f.f(aaf)$$

since using the latter we can compute fix points by reduction:

$$Y_T F = AAF = (\lambda a.\lambda f.f(aaf))AF \rightarrow_\beta (\lambda f.f(AAf))F \rightarrow_\beta F(AAF) = F(Y_T F)$$

The term Y_T is usually called Turing's fix point combinator and has the property that, for all terms M, $Y_T M \rightarrow_\beta^* M(Y_T M)$, as shown above. Thanks to this property, we can use Y_T to define recursive functions. For example, consider the following definition of a term H:

$$H = \lambda f.\lambda n.IF\,(\textit{is-zero? }n)\;THEN\;\overline{1}\;ELSE\;(MULT\,n\,(f(PRED\,n)))$$

Now the factorial function can be defined as the fix point of H:

$$FACT = Y_T\;H$$

We then have the reduction sequence

$$FACT\,\overline{n} \;=\; Y_T H \overline{n} \;\rightarrow_\beta^*\; H(Y_T H)\overline{n} \;\rightarrow_\beta^*$$
$$IF\ (\textit{is-zero?}\ \overline{n})\ THEN\ \overline{1}\ ELSE\ (MULT\ \overline{n}\ (Y_T H(PRED\ \overline{n})))$$

where $Y_T H(PRED\ \overline{n})$ is, by our definition, $FACT(PRED\ \overline{n})$, as required.

Thus, although functions in the λ-calculus are anonymous, we can simulate a recursive "call" using a fix point operator. This is a technique that we can use to define recursive functions in general.

3.6 Functional programming

The work done by Church on abstract computation models based on the mathematical theory of functions has had a deep influence on the design of modern *functional* programming languages. The λ-calculus can be seen as the abstract model of computation underlying functional programming languages such as LISP, Scheme, ML, and Haskell.

The main domains of application for functional languages up to now have been in artificial intelligence (for the implementation of expert systems), text processing (for instance, the UNIX editor emacs is implemented in LISP), graphical interfaces, natural language, telephony, music composition, symbolic mathematical systems, theorem provers, and proof assistants.

When developing software applications, properties such as low maintenance cost, easy debugging, or formally provable correctness nowadays have a high priority. For example, in safety-critical domains (such as medical applications, telecommunications, or transport systems) it is important to develop programs whose *correctness* can be certified (i.e., formally proved). Functional languages are a good alternative to imperative languages in this case since functional programs are in general shorter and are easier to debug and maintain than their imperative counterparts. For these reasons, functional programming languages are becoming increasingly popular.

LISP, introduced by John McCarthy in the 1950s, is considered to be the ancestor of all functional programming languages. The syntax of LISP is based on lists (as the name of the language suggests: *LISt Processing*), and the atomic elements of lists are numbers and characters. Its conciseness and elegance have made LISP a very popular language. Since data and programs are represented as lists, it is easy in LISP to define *higher-order functions* (that is, functions that take other functions as their argument or produce functions as their result). This style of programming is one of the main features of functional languages. Several versions of LISP are in use, including Scheme.

Modern functional languages such as ML and Haskell have radically changed the syntax and introduced sophisticated type systems with type inference capabilities. These modern functional languages are still based on the λ-calculus, but their design is also influenced by the theory of recursive functions developed by Gödel and Kleene, which we discuss in the next chapter. We will come back to the relationship between functional programming languages and abstract computation models at the end of the next chapter.

3.7 Further reading

More information on the λ-calculus can be found in [21]. Barendregt's book [4] is a comprehensive reference. For an introduction to functional programming we recommend the books by Bird [6] and by Cousineau and Mauny [10]. For a description of the functional languages mentioned above, see the following references: LISP [32], Scheme [50], ML [35], and Haskell [51].

3.8 Exercises

1. Compute the sets of free and bound variables for the terms in Example 3.2.

2. Write the result of the following substitutions.

   a) $x\{y \mapsto M\}$, where M is an arbitrary λ-term

   b) $(\lambda x.xy)\{y \mapsto (xx)\}$

   c) $(\lambda y.xy)\{y \mapsto (xx)\}$

   d) $(xx)\{x \mapsto \lambda y.y\}$

3. Compute the normal forms of the following terms

   a) $\lambda y.(\lambda x.x)y$

   b) $\lambda y.y(\lambda x.x)$

   c) II

   d) KI

   e) KKK

   where $K = \lambda xy.x$ and $I = \lambda x.x$.

4. Different notions of normal form were discussed in this chapter, including the full normal form (or simply normal form) and weak head normal form.

   a) What is the difference between a term having a normal form and being a normal form? Write down some example terms.

   b) If a closed term is a weak head normal form, it has to be an abstraction $\lambda x.M$. Why?

   c) Indicate whether the following λ-terms have a normal form:

      - $(\lambda x.(\lambda y.yx)z)v$

      - $(\lambda x.xxy)(\lambda x.xxy)$

   d) Show that the term $\Omega = (\lambda x.xx)(\lambda x.xx)$ does not have a normal form. Find a term different from Ω that is not normalising (i.e., a term such that every reduction sequence starting from it is infinite).

5. Explain why if a reduction system is confluent, then each term has at most one normal form.

6. Show leftmost-outermost and leftmost-innermost reductions for the following terms:

   - $G\ (F\ x)$ where

   $$G\ =\ \lambda x.xxx$$
   $$F\ =\ \lambda yz.yz$$

   - $\Theta\Theta\Theta$

   - $\Theta(\Theta\Theta)$

   where

   $$\Theta\ =\ \lambda x.xKSK$$
   $$S\ =\ \lambda xyz.xz(yz)$$
   $$K\ =\ \lambda xy.x$$

7. In your view, which are the best and worst reduction strategies for a functional programming language? Give examples to support your claims.

8. In this chapter, we have shown how to define arithmetic operations using Church numerals.

   a) Check that the term $ADD = \lambda xyab.(xa)(yab)$ behaves like the addition function; that is, show that when we apply ADD to two Church numerals, we obtain the Church numeral representing their sum.

   Hint: Reduce the term $(\lambda x.\lambda y.\lambda a.\lambda b.(xa)(yab))\overline{n}\,\overline{m}$.

   b) Show that the λ-term $MULT = \lambda x.\lambda y.\lambda z.x(yz)$ applied to two Church numerals $\overline{m}$ and $\overline{n}$ computes their product $\overline{m \times n}$.

   c) Which arithmetic operation does the term $\lambda n.\lambda m.m \ (MULT\,n) \ \overline{1}$ compute?

9. Check that the following definitions are correct by applying them to the Boolean constants:

$AND = \lambda x.\lambda y.x \ y \ x$

$OR = \lambda x.\lambda y.x \ x \ y$

10. Consider the model of computation defined as the restriction of the λ-calculus to the set of *linear* terms. Linear terms are inductively defined as follows:

   − A variable is a linear term.

   − If x occurs free in a linear term M, then $\lambda x.M$ is a linear term.

   − If M and N are linear terms and the sets of free variables of M and N are disjoint, then $(M \ N)$ is a linear term.

In $\lambda x.M$, the variable x is bound; terms are defined modulo α-equivalence as usual.

   a) Show that $\lambda x.\lambda y.xy$ is a linear term according to the definition above, and give an example of a non-linear term.

   b) The computation rule in the linear λ-calculus is the standard β-reduction rule. Indicate whether each of the following statements is true or false and why.

     i. In the linear λ-calculus, we can ignore α-equivalence when we apply the β-reduction rule.

     ii. If we β-reduce a linear term, we obtain another linear term.

     iii. The linear λ-calculus is confluent.

     iv. Every sequence of reductions in the linear λ-calculus is finite (in other words, the linear λ-calculus is terminating).

     v. The linear λ-calculus is a Turing-complete model of computation.

11. Combinatory logic (CL for short) is a universal model of computation. Terms in the language of CL are built out of variables $x, y, \ldots$, constants S and K, and applications $(M \ N)$. More precisely, terms are generated by the grammar

$$M, N ::= x \mid S \mid K \mid (M \ N)$$

The standard notational conventions are used to avoid brackets: Applications associate to the left, and we do not write the outermost brackets. For instance, we write $K\,x\,y$ for the term $((K\,x)\,y)$.

There are two computation rules in combinatory logic:

$$
\begin{aligned}
K\,x\,y &\rightarrow x \\
S\,x\,y\,z &\rightarrow x\,z\,(y\,z)
\end{aligned}
$$

a) Using the rules above, there is a sequence of reduction steps

$$SKKx \rightarrow^* x$$

Show all the reduction steps in this sequence.

b) The term SKK can be seen as the implementation of the identity function in this system since, for any argument x, the term $SKKx$ evaluates to x.

Show that SKM, where M is an arbitrary term, also defines the identity function.

c) Consider the system of combinatory logic without the second computation rule (that is, only the rule $Kxy \rightarrow x$ may be used). We call this weaker system CL^-.

We call CL^+ the system of combinatory logic with an additional constant I and rule $Ix \rightarrow x$.

Indicate whether each of the following statements is true or false and why.

   i. In CL^-, all the reduction sequences are finite.

   ii. The system CL^+ has the same computational power as the system CL.

   iii. The system CL^- is Turing complete.

4
Recursive Functions

In the previous chapters, we discussed the notion of a computable function and characterised this class of functions as the ones that can be defined via Turing machines or the λ-calculus. In this chapter, we give an alternative characterisation of computable functions based on the notion of a recursive function. Usually, we say that a function is recursive if it "calls itself". Recursive functions are functions for which the result for a certain argument depends on the results obtained for other (smaller in some sense) arguments. Recursion is a very useful tool in modern programming languages, in particular when dealing with inductive data structures such as lists, trees, etc.

The theory of recursive functions was developed by Kurt Gödel and Stephen Kleene in the 1930s. In this chapter, we will define the general class of *partial recursive functions*. These are functions on numbers, each one with a fixed arity; that is, with a specific number of arguments. In the definition of recursive functions, we will identify some basic functions that serve as building blocks in our characterisation of computability. We will also identify some mechanisms that can be used to combine functions, so that starting from the basic initial functions we can obtain a class of functions that is equivalent to the class of functions that can be defined, for instance, in the λ-calculus.

Primitive recursive functions play an important role in the formalisation of computability. Intuitively speaking, partial recursive functions are those that can be computed by Turing machines, whereas primitive recursive functions can be computed by a specific class of Turing machines that always halt. Many of the functions normally studied in arithmetic are primitive recursive. Addition, subtraction, multiplication, division, factorial, and exponential are just some of the most familiar examples of primitive recursive functions. Ackermann's function, which we will define in Section 4.1, is a well-known example of a non-primitive recursive function.

There are several alternative definitions of the class of primitive recursive functions. There is no consensus as to what is the best set of basic initial functions, and also the notion of recursion may vary; for instance, in some cases, a notion of iteration is used instead of recursion. As with the variants of Turing machines mentioned in Chapter 2, it can be shown that the alternative definitions of primitive recursion available in the literature are all equivalent.

We start the chapter by defining the class of primitive recursive functions as the least set including the zero, successor, and projection functions and closed under the operations of composition and primitive recursion. We then go on to define more general recursive functions using a minimisation scheme. We finish this chapter with a discussion of functional programming and partial recursive functions.

4.1 Primitive recursive functions

In the definition of primitive recursive functions, we will use the natural numbers, together with some basic projection functions to erase, copy, and permute arguments of functions. Starting from these basic functions, we will use two mechanisms to define more interesting functions: composition and the primitive recursive scheme. All the functions that we will define work on the set of natural numbers, denoted Nat. Thus, a function of arity k will take k natural numbers as arguments and produce a result of type Nat. This is abbreviated as

$$f : \mathsf{Nat}^k \rightarrow \mathsf{Nat}.$$

Composition is a familiar operation. Given two functions f and g from Nat to Nat, we can define a new function h so that the result of h on a number x is obtained by applying f to the result of g on x; that is, $h(x) = f(g(x))$. The composition operator used in the definition of primitive recursive functions is more general than this, as we will see below.

Primitive recursion is possibly the easiest way to define recursive functions. The idea is that, to define a function f, first we give the value of f for 0, and then for any other number $n + 1$ we define $f(n + 1)$ in terms of $f(n)$. For example, the factorial function is usually defined by the equations

$$0! = 1 \quad \text{and} \quad (n + 1)! = (n + 1) * n!$$

We see that, in the second equation, to compute the factorial of $n + 1$ we use multiplication and the factorial of n. The primitive recursive scheme, defined below, generalises this technique. Before giving the definition of primitive recursive functions, we introduce some notation.

Notation. We use $x_1, \ldots, y_1, \ldots$ to denote natural numbers, f, g, h to represent functions, and $X_1, X_2, \ldots$ to represent tuples or sequences of the form $x_1, \ldots, x_n$. We only have tuples on natural numbers; thus we will work modulo associativity for simplicity: $(X_1, (x_1, x_2), X_2) = (X_1, x_1, x_2, X_2)$.

Definition 4.1 (Primitive recursive functions)

A function $f : \mathsf{Nat}^k \to \mathsf{Nat}$ is primitive recursive if it can be defined from a set of initial functions using composition and the primitive recursive scheme. The set of initial functions and the composition and recursive scheme are defined below.

– *Initial functions:* These can be either the zero and successor functions, used to build natural numbers, or projections. More precisely:

1. The constant function zero, written 0, and the successor function S are initial functions. Natural numbers can be built from these two functions using composition. We write n or $\mathsf{S}^n(0)$ for $\underbrace{\mathsf{S}(\ldots \mathsf{S}(\mathsf{S}(0)\ldots))}_{n}$.

2. *Projection functions:* These are functions that allow us to select an element of a tuple. There are projection functions for tuples of any length. We will denote by π_i^n the function that selects the ith element of a tuple of length n. More precisely,

$$\pi_i^n(x_1, \ldots, x_n) = x_i \quad (1 \leq i \leq n)$$

We will omit the superindex, writing simply π_i, when there is no ambiguity.

– Composition allows us to define a primitive recursive function h using auxiliary functions $f, g_1, \ldots, g_n$, where $n \geq 0$:

$$h(X) = f(g_1(X), \ldots, g_n(X))$$

– The primitive recursive scheme allows us to define a recursive function h using two auxiliary primitive recursive functions f, g. The function h is defined as follows:

$$
\begin{aligned}
h(X, 0) &= f(X) \\
h(X, \mathsf{S}(n)) &= g(X, h(X, n), n).
\end{aligned}
$$

There are two cases in the definition of h above, depending on whether the last argument is 0 or not. If it is 0, then the value of $h(X, 0)$ is obtained by computing $f(X)$. Otherwise, the second equation defines h by using the auxiliary function g and the result of a recursive call to h.

According to Definition 4.1, any function that can be specified by using initial functions and an arbitrary (finite) number of operations of composition and primitive recursion is primitive recursive. We give examples of primitive recursive functions below.

As we have already mentioned, there are alternative versions of the primitive recursion scheme. For instance, the one above could be replaced by a more restricted iteration scheme.

Definition 4.2

Let g be a primitive recursive function. The following scheme, defining the function h in terms of g, is called *pure iteration*:

$$\begin{aligned} h(X, 0) &= X \\ h(X, \mathsf{S}(n)) &= g(h(X, n)) \end{aligned}$$

The function h defined by the pure iteration scheme, using the auxiliary function g, takes X and a number n and iterates n times the function g on X. For this reason, we can abbreviate $h(X, n)$ as $g^n(X)$.

We do not have constant functions of the form $C(X) = n$ as initial functions in Definition 4.1. However, we can see 0 as a constant function with no arguments, and every other constant function can be built by composition using 0 and S, as shown in the following example.

Example 4.3

The constant function $zero(x, y) = 0$ is defined as an instance of the composition scheme using the initial 0-ary function 0. The constant function $one(x, y) = \mathsf{S}(zero(x, y))$ is again an instance of the composition scheme.

Functions obtained from primitive recursive functions by introducing "dummy" arguments, permuting arguments, or repeating them are also primitive recursive. To keep our definitions simple, we will sometimes omit the definition of those functions.

Example 4.4

Consider the standard functions add and mul from Nat^2 to Nat:

$$\text{add}(x, y) = x + y \quad \text{mul}(x, y) = x * y$$

The function add can be defined by primitive recursion as

$$
\begin{aligned}
\text{add}(x, 0) &= f(x) \\
\text{add}(x, \text{S}(n)) &= g(x, \text{add}(x, n), n)
\end{aligned}
$$

where

$$
\begin{aligned}
f(x) &= \pi_1(x) &= x \\
g(x_1, x_2, x_3) &= \text{S}(\pi_2(x_1, x_2, x_3)) &= \text{S}(x_2)
\end{aligned}
$$

The primitive recursive function mul is defined by

$$
\begin{aligned}
\text{mul}(x, 0) &= f(x) \\
\text{mul}(x, \text{S}(n)) &= g(x, \text{mul}(x, n), n)
\end{aligned}
$$

where

$$
\begin{aligned}
f(x) &= 0 \\
g(x_1, x_2, x_3) &= \text{add}(\pi_1(x_1, x_2, x_3), \pi_2(x_1, x_2, x_3)) &= \text{add}(x_1, x_2)
\end{aligned}
$$

Similarly, we can define the function sub to subtract numbers.

$$
\begin{aligned}
\text{sub}(x, 0) &= \pi_1(x) \\
\text{sub}(x, \text{S}(n)) &= \text{pred}(x, \text{sub}(x, n), n)
\end{aligned}
$$

where the function pred is defined below using projections and the function predecessor (defined by primitive recursion).

$$
\begin{aligned}
\text{pred}(x, y, z) &= \text{predecessor}(\pi_2(x, y, z)) \\
\text{predecessor}(0) &= 0 \\
\text{predecessor}(\text{S}(n)) &= \pi_2(\text{predecessor}(n), n)
\end{aligned}
$$

Functions defined by cases may be more difficult to encode directly using primitive recursion. In order to be able to express definitions by cases in a convenient way, we introduce the notion of a recursive predicate.

Definition 4.5 (Primitive recursive predicates)

The condition P depending on $X \in \text{Nat}^n$, such that $P(X)$ is either true or false, is called an *n-ary predicate*. An n-ary predicate P is primitive recursive if its *characteristic function* $\mathcal{X}_P : \text{Nat}^n \to \{0, 1\}$ is primitive recursive. The characteristic function of a predicate associates 1 with the tuples X for which $P(X)$ holds and 0 with the others.

Example 4.6

The predicates eq (equality) and lt (less than) are primitive recursive with characteristic functions

$$
\begin{aligned}
\mathcal{X}_{\text{lt}}(x, y) &= f(\text{sub}(y, x)) \\
\mathcal{X}_{\text{eq}}(x, y) &= f(\text{add}(\text{sub}(x, y), \text{sub}(y, x)))
\end{aligned}
$$

where $f(0) = 0$ and $f(\text{S}(n)) = 1$. The function f is primitive recursive (see the exercises at the end of the chapter).

Definition 4.7 (Case construction)

If $f_1, \ldots, f_k$ are primitive recursive functions from Nat^n to Nat, $P_1, \ldots, P_k$ are primitive recursive n-ary predicates, and for every $X \in \text{Nat}^n$ exactly one of the conditions $P_1(X), \ldots, P_k(X)$ is true, then the function $f : \text{Nat}^n \to \text{Nat}$ defined below is primitive recursive.

$$
f(X) = \begin{cases}
f_1(X) & \text{if } P_1(X) \\
f_2(X) & \text{if } P_2(X) \\
\ldots \\
f_k(X) & \text{if } P_k(X)
\end{cases}
$$

We can easily understand how such a function can be built from primitive recursive functions. Since exactly one of the conditions $P_1(X), \ldots, P_k(X)$ is true, then exactly one of the values of $\mathcal{X}_{P_i}(X)$ will be 1 and all the others will be 0. Then one can obtain the function f by composition using $P_1, \ldots, P_k$, the given functions $f_1, \ldots, f_k$, addition, and multiplication (the latter two denoted by $+$ and $*$).

$$
f(X) = f_1(X) * \mathcal{X}_{P_1}(X) + \cdots + f_k(X) * \mathcal{X}_{P_k}(X)
$$

Thus, f is a primitive recursive function.

For example, we can give a definition by cases for the operator of *bounded minimisation*. This operator searches for the minimum number that satisfies a given condition, in a given interval, where the condition is specified as a primitive recursive predicate. To show that bounded minimisation is primitive recursive, we can define it as follows.

Definition 4.8

Let P be an $(n + 1)$-ary primitive recursive predicate and $X \in \text{Nat}^n$. The *bounded minimisation* of P is the primitive recursive function

$$m_P(X, k) = \begin{cases} \min\{y \mid 0 \leq y \leq k \text{ and } P(X, y)\} & \text{if the set is not empty} \\ k + 1 & \text{otherwise} \end{cases}$$

All the primitive recursive functions are total; that is, for any primitive recursive function $f : \mathsf{Nat}^k \to \mathsf{Nat}$, given k numbers $n_1, \ldots, n_k$, the value $f(n_1, \ldots, n_k)$ is well defined. This can be proved as follows.

Proof

The initial functions are obviously total, as is the composition of two total functions.

Assume h is defined by primitive recursion using two total functions f and g. We can prove by induction on n that $h(X, n)$ is total for all n. First, note that $h(X, 0)$ is total (since f is). Next, assume that $h(X, n)$ is well defined (induction hypothesis). Then, since g is total, $h(X, \mathsf{S}(n))$ is also well-defined.   □

Although most of the functions that we use are primitive recursive, the set of computable functions also includes functions that are outside this class. For instance, some computable functions are partial functions, and there are also total computable functions that are not primitive recursive. Ackermann's function is a standard example of a total, non-primitive recursive function:

$$\begin{aligned} ack(0, n) &= \mathsf{S}(n) \\ ack(\mathsf{S}(n), 0) &= ack(n, \mathsf{S}(0)) \\ ack(\mathsf{S}(n), \mathsf{S}(m)) &= ack(n, ack(\mathsf{S}(n), m)) \end{aligned}$$

In the next section, we define the class of partial recursive functions by including an additional mechanism to build functions, called unbounded minimisation or just minimisation.

4.2 Partial recursive functions

We start by defining the unbounded minimisation operator.

Definition 4.9 (Minimisation)

Let f be a total function from Nat^{n+1} to Nat. The function g from Nat^n to Nat that computes for each tuple X of numbers the minimum y such that $f(X, y)$

is zero is called the minimisation of f. More precisely, the *minimisation* of f is the function g defined as follows:

$$g(X) = \min\{y \mid f(X, y) = 0\}$$

We denote g as M_f.

Note that although the equality predicate used in the definition of minimisation is total, the minimisation operation is not necessarily terminating. It requires performing a search without an upper limit on the set of numbers to be considered. For this reason, a function defined by minimisation of a total function may be partial.

The class of *partial recursive functions* includes the primitive recursive functions and also functions defined by minimisation. Despite its name, this class also includes total functions. We will simply call the functions in this class *recursive functions*.

Definition 4.10 (Recursive functions)

The set of *recursive functions* is defined as the smallest set of functions containing the natural numbers (built from 0 and the successor function S) and the projection functions and closed by composition, primitive recursion, and minimisation.

Closure by minimisation implies that, for every $n \geq 0$ and every total recursive function $f : \mathsf{Nat}^{n+1} \to \mathsf{Nat}$, the function $M_f : \mathsf{Nat}^n \to \mathsf{Nat}$ defined by

$$M_f(X) = \min\{y \mid f(X, y) = 0\}$$

is a (possibly partial) recursive function. In other words, a function is recursive if it can be defined using initial functions and a finite number of operations of composition, primitive recursion, and minimisation.

In particular, every primitive recursive function is also recursive (since in both definitions we use the same initial functions, composition, and primitive recursive scheme). However, if minimisation is used in the definition of the function, the result may not be primitive recursive, and it may fail to be total.

Kleene showed the following result, which indicates that only one minimisation operation is sufficient to define recursive functions.

Theorem 4.11 (Kleene normal form)

Let h be a (possibly partial) recursive function on Nat^k. Then, a number n can be found such that

$$h(x_1, \ldots, x_k) = f(M_g(n, x_1, \ldots, x_k))$$

where f and g are primitive recursive functions.

Although all the functions we have defined are functions from numbers to numbers, the primitive recursion and minimisation mechanisms can also be used to define functions on strings, lists, trees, etc. Indeed, using a technique developed by Gödel, known as Gödel numbering, it is possible to associate a number (i.e., a *code*) with each string, list, tree, etc., and then define the functions on data structures as numeric functions acting on codes. Instead of encoding the data, we can redefine the initial functions, composition, recursive schemes, and minimisation to work directly on the specific data structure of interest.

We finish this section by stating, without a proof, that all the partial recursive functions can be defined in the λ-calculus. The converse is also true; indeed, these two models of computation are equivalent (and also equivalent in computational power to Turing machines).

Property 4.12

The set of recursive functions, the set of functions that can be defined in the λ-calculus, and the set of functions that can be computed by a Turing machine coincide.

4.3 Programming with functions

The common feature of all functional programming languages is that programs consist of *functions* (as in the mathematical notion of a function, which is the basis of the λ-calculus and the theory of partial recursive functions; not to be confused with the notion of a function used in imperative languages).

Most modern functional programming languages are *strongly typed* (that is, equipped with a type system that guarantees that well-typed expressions will not produce type errors at run time) and have built-in memory management. ML and Haskell are examples of these. In the rest of this section, we give examples of functional definitions using the syntax of Haskell.

A function in this sense is simply a mapping between elements of two sets, for instance,

$$f :: \alpha \rightarrow \beta$$

can be seen as a declaration of a function f that, applied to an argument x in α, gives a result $(f\ x)$ in β.[1] With this approach, the focus is on *what* is to be computed, not *how* it should be computed. In the example above, we say that the function f has *type* $\alpha \rightarrow \beta$.

Some functional programming languages adopt a syntactic style that is based on equational definitions similar to the definitions of primitive recursive functions or, more generally, partial recursive functions. However, functional languages also allow the programmer to define anonymous functions, as in the λ-calculus. In general, a function in a functional programming language can be defined in terms of other functions previously defined by the programmer, taken from the libraries, or provided as language primitives. Composition of functions and recursion play major roles in functional programming languages.

The *composition* operator, denoted by $\cdot$, as in the expression f $\cdot$ g, is itself a function; it is predefined in functional languages. In Haskell, it is defined as follows:

```
·  ::  ((β → γ), (α → β)) → (α → γ)
(f · g) x = f (g x)
```

The type of $\cdot$ indicates that we can only compose functions whose types are compatible. In other words, the composition operator $\cdot$ expects two functions, f and g, as arguments, such that the domain of f coincides with the co-domain of g. The type of f is $(\beta \rightarrow \gamma)$ and the type of g is $(\alpha \rightarrow \beta)$, where α, β, and γ are type variables representing arbitrary types.

The result of composing two functions f and g of compatible types $(\beta \rightarrow \gamma)$ and $(\alpha \rightarrow \beta)$, respectively, is a function of type $(\alpha \rightarrow \gamma)$. It accepts an argument x of type α (which will be supplied to g) and produces f (g x), which is in the co-domain of f and therefore is of type γ.

Example 4.13 (Composition)

Consider the function

```
square :: Integer → Integer
```

that computes the square of a number. It can be defined by the equation

```
square x = x * x
```

where we have used a predefined multiplication operator, written *.

----

[1] Most functional languages adopt the λ-calculus notation $(f\ x)$ for application.

Using the function `square` and the composition operator, we can define a function `quad` that computes the fourth power of a number as follows:

```
quad = square · square
```

Arithmetic operations are built-in functions used in infix notation, as in the expressions `3 + 4` or `x * x`. In Haskell, we can use them in prefix notation if we enclose them in brackets; for example, `(+) 3 4`.

The functions `(+)` and `+` have different types:

```
+ :: (Integer, Integer) → Integer
```

```
(+) :: Integer → Integer → Integer
```

The function `(+)` is the *Curryfied* version of `+`; that is, instead of working on *pairs* of numbers (i.e., two numbers provided simultaneously), it expects a number followed by another number. This might seem a small difference at first sight, but Curryfication (the word derives from the name of the mathematician Haskell Curry, after whom the programming language also is named) provides great flexibility to functional languages. For instance, we can use `(*)`, the Curryfied version of the multiplication operator, to define a function `double`, which doubles its argument:

```
double :: Integer → Integer
double = (*) 2
```

As in the λ-calculus, there are some notational conventions to avoid writing too many brackets in expressions; for example, it is understood that application has priority over arithmetic operations. For example, `square 1 + 4 * 2` should be read as `(square 1) + (4 * 2)`.

The process of evaluating an expression is a *simplification process*, also called a *reduction process*. An evaluator for a functional programming language implements the β-reduction rule of the λ-calculus. The goal is to obtain the *value* or irreducible form (also called the *normal form*) associated with an expression by a series of reduction steps. The *meaning* of an expression is its value.

Functional programming languages inherit their main properties from the λ-calculus. One of the main properties is the *unicity of normal forms:*

> In (pure) functional languages, the value of an expression is uniquely determined by its components.

An obvious advantage of this property is improved readability of programs.

Not all the reduction sequences that start with a given expression lead to a value. This is not in contradiction with the previous property. It is caused by non-termination. Some reduction sequences for a given expression may be infinite, but all the sequences that terminate reach the same value. This is more clearly seen with an example.

Example 4.14 (Non-termination)

Let us define the constant function `fortytwo`. This is a primitive recursive function, and in a language like Haskell we can define it with an equation:

```
fortytwo x = 42
```

We can also define equationally a non-primitive recursive function `infinity`:

```
infinity = infinity + 1
```

It is clear that the evaluation of `infinity` never reaches a normal form. The expression

`fortytwo infinity`

gives rise to some reduction sequences that do not terminate, but those that terminate give the value 42 (unicity of normal forms).

The example above shows that, although the normal form is unique, the order of reductions is important. As in the λ-calculus, functional programming languages evaluate expressions by reduction and follow a given evaluation strategy. Recall that a *strategy of evaluation* specifies the order in which reductions take place; in other words, it defines the reduction sequence that the language implements.

The most popular strategies of evaluation for functional languages are:

1. *Call-by-name (normal order):* In the presence of a function application, first the definition of the function is used and then the arguments are evaluated if needed.

2. *Call-by-value (applicative order):* In the presence of a function application, first the arguments are evaluated and then the definition of the function is used to evaluate the application.

For example, using call-by-name, the expression `fortytwo infinity` is reduced in one step to the value 42 since this strategy specifies that the definition of the function `fortytwo` is used, which does not require the argument (it is a constant function). However, when using call-by-value, we must first evaluate the argument `infinity`, and, as we already mentioned, the reduction sequence for this expression is infinite; hence we will never reach a normal form. Call-by-name guarantees that if an expression has a value, it will be reached.

As this example shows, different strategies of evaluation require different numbers of reduction steps, and therefore the efficiency of a program (which is related to the number of reduction steps) depends on the strategy used. Some functional languages (for instance, ML) use call-by-value so that when an argument is used several times in the definition of a function it is evaluated only once. Haskell uses a strategy called *lazy evaluation*. It is based on call-by-name, which guarantees that if an expression has a normal form, the evaluator will find it, but to avoid the potential lack of efficiency of a pure call-by-name strategy, Haskell uses a *sharing* mechanism. When an argument is used many times in a function definition, its evaluation is performed *at most once*, and the value is shared between all its occurrences.

4.4 Further reading

There are many books and journal articles on recursive functions, for instance [18, 19, 39, 46, 2]. Some of these references provide alternative definitions of the classes of primitive recursive functions and general recursive functions. Kleene's book [27] is an interesting reference. To complement the information on Haskell given in the previous section, we recommend [6, 51].

4.5 Exercises

1. Show that the factorial function is primitive recursive.

2. Show that the function f used in Example 4.6, defined by $f(0) = 0$ and $f(\mathsf{S}(n)) = 1$, is primitive recursive.

3. Consider the functions Div and Mod such that $Div(x, y)$ and $Mod(x, y)$ compute the quotient and remainder, respectively, of the division of x by y. These are not total functions because division by 0 is not defined, but we can complete the definition by stating that $Div(x, 0) = 0$ and $Mod(x, 0) = x$. Show that the extended functions Div and Mod are primitive recursive.

4. Show that the pure iteration scheme given in Definition 4.2 is equivalent

to the primitive recursive scheme given in Definition 4.1.

5. Indicate whether the following statements are true or false:

   a) All primitive recursive functions are total.

   b) All total computable functions are primitive recursive.

   c) All partial recursive functions are computable.

   d) All total functions are computable.

6. Write functional programs defining `cube` (the function that computes the third power of a number) and `double` (the function that doubles its argument). Describe the reduction sequences for the expression

$$\texttt{cube (double (3 + 1))}$$

   using call-by-name (normal order) and call-by-value (applicative order).

7. In functional languages, there is a primitive function `if-then-else` that we can use to define a function by cases that depend on a Boolean condition (see the case construction in Definition 4.7). Thus,

   `if x == 0 then 0 else x * y`

   will return 0 if the value of `x` is equal to 0 and will return the product of `x` and `y` otherwise.

   Assume the function `mult` on natural numbers is defined by

   `mult x y` $\stackrel{\text{def}}{=}$ `if x == 0 then 0 else x * y`

   where `==` is the equality test. Assume that e_1 `==` e_2 is evaluated by reducing e_1 and e_2 to normal form and then comparing the normal forms.

   a) Is `mult` commutative over numbers; i.e., will `mult m n` and `mult n m` compute the same result for all numbers m and n?

   b) Let `infinity` be the function defined by

      `infinity` $\stackrel{\text{def}}{=}$ `infinity + 1`

      What is the value of `mult infinity 0`?

      What is the value of `mult 0 infinity`?

5

Logic-Based Models of Computation

During the late 1920s, Jacques Herbrand, a young mathematician, developed a method to check the validity of a class of first-order logic formulas. In his thesis, published in 1931, Herbrand discussed what can be considered the first unification procedure. Unification is at the heart of modern implementations of logic programming languages.

In this chapter, we will discuss the model of computation that serves as a basis for the logic programming paradigm. Prolog, one of the most popular logic programming languages, will be discussed in the final part of the chapter.

5.1 The Herbrand universe

In logic programs, the domain of computation is the *Herbrand universe*, the set of *terms* defined over a universal *alphabet* of

- *variables*, such as X, Y, etc., and

- *function symbols* with fixed arities (the arity of a symbol is as usual the number of arguments associated with it).

   Function symbols are usually denoted by $f, g, h, \ldots$, or $a, b, c, \ldots$ if the arity is 0 (i.e., $a, b, c, \ldots$ denote constants). In our examples, we will often use more meaningful names for function symbols.

Definition 5.1 (Terms)

A *term* is either a variable or has the form $f(t_1, \ldots, t_n)$, where f is a function symbol of arity n and $t_1, \ldots, t_n$ are terms. Notice that n may be 0, and in this case we will just write f, omitting the brackets.

Example 5.2

If a is a constant, f a binary function, and g a unary function, then $f(f(X, g(a)), Y)$ is a term, where X and Y are variables.

Function symbols in this framework correspond to data constructors; they are used to give structure to the domain of computation. For example, if our algorithm deals with arrays of three elements, a suitable data structure can be defined using a function symbol array of arity 3. The array containing the elements $0, 1, 2$ is then represented by the term array$(0, 1, 2)$.

There is no definition associated with a function symbol (although in Prolog implementations there are some built-in functions, such as arithmetic operations, that have a specific meaning).

We will not fix the alphabet used to define the Herbrand universe. The names of variables and function symbols needed to represent the problem domain can be freely chosen. In this chapter, names of variables start with capital letters and names of functions start with lower case letters (we follow the conventions used in Prolog's syntax).

5.2 Logic programs

Once the domain of computation is established, a problem can be described by means of logic formulas involving *predicates*.

Predicates represent properties of terms and are used to build basic formulas that are then composed using operators such as *and, not,* and *or,* denoted by $\land, \neg,$ and $\lor$, respectively.

Definition 5.3

Let $\mathcal{P}$ be a set of *predicate symbols*, each with a fixed arity. If p is a predicate of arity n and $t_1, \ldots, t_n$ are terms, then $p(t_1, \ldots, t_n)$ is an *atomic formula*, or simply an *atom*. Again, n may be 0, and in this case we omit the brackets. A *literal* is an atomic formula or a negated atomic formula.

Example 5.4

The following are two literals (the second is a negated atom), where we use the predicates `value` of arity 2 and `raining` of arity 0, a unary function symbol `number`, and the constant 1:

```
value(number(1),1)
¬raining
```

We have followed another syntactic convention of Prolog in that names of predicates start with a lower case letter.

We mentioned before that logic (or, more precisely, a subset of first-order logic) can be seen as an abstract model of computation. Logic formulas will be used to express algorithms or, more generally, partial functions (since some of the computations that we will model may not halt). We will call them *logic programs*. As another piece of evidence to support Church's Thesis, it can be shown that logic programs can express exactly the same class of functions that Turing machines can define. Logic programs are Turing complete.

Definition 5.5 (Logic programs)

Logic programs are sets of *definite clauses*, also called *Horn clauses*, that are a restricted class of first-order formulas. A *definite clause* is a disjunction of literals with at most one positive literal.

We now introduce some notational conventions for clauses. We write P_1, $P_2, \ldots$ to denote atoms. A definite clause $P_1 \vee \neg P_2 \vee \ldots \vee \neg P_n$ (where P_1 is the only positive literal) will be written

$$P_1 \; :- \; P_2, \ldots, P_n.$$

and we read it as

$$\text{``}P_1 \text{ if } P_2 \text{ and } \ldots \text{ and } P_n.\text{''}$$

We call P_1 the *head* of the clause and $P_2, \ldots, P_n$ the *body*.

If the clause contains just P_1 and no negative literals, then we write

$$P_1.$$

Both kinds of clauses are called *program clauses*; the first kind is called a *rule* and the second kind is called a *fact*. If the clause contains only negative literals, we call it a *goal* or *query* and write

$$:-P_2, \ldots, P_n.$$

Program clauses can be seen as defining a database: Facts specify information to be stored, and rules indicate how we can deduce more information from the previously defined data.

Goals are questions to be answered using the information about the problem in the database. This can be better seen with some examples.

Example 5.6

In the following logic program, the first four clauses are facts and the last one is a rule.

```
based(prolog,logic).¹
based(haskell,functions).
likes(claire,functions).
likes(max,logic).
likes(X,L) :- based(L,Y), likes(X,Y).
```

Here we have used two binary predicates, based and likes, constants prolog, logic, haskell, functions, claire, and max, and variables X, Y, and L.

The first two clauses in the program can be read as "Prolog is based on logic and Haskell on functions". More precisely, these are facts about the predicate based; they define a relation to be stored in the database.

The next three clauses define the predicate likes. There are two facts, which can be read as "Claire likes functions and Max likes logic", and a rule that allows us to deduce more information about people's tastes. We can read this rule as "X likes L if L is based on Y and X likes Y".

Once this information is specified in the program as shown above, we can ask questions such as "Is there somebody (some Z) who likes Prolog?" which corresponds to the goal

```
:- likes(Z,prolog).
```

With the information given in the program, we can deduce that Max likes Prolog. We know that Max likes logic and Prolog is based on logic, and therefore the last rule allows us to conclude that Max likes Prolog.

The precise deduction mechanism that we use to reach this conclusion can be specified using an inference rule called *resolution*, which we describe below.

---

[1] In some versions of Prolog, the word prolog is reserved; therefore, to run this example, it might be necessary to replace prolog by myprolog, for instance.

5.2.1 Answers

Answers to goals will be represented by *substitutions* that associate values with the unknowns (i.e., the variables) in the goal. *Values* are also terms in the Herbrand universe (see Definition 5.1).

Definition 5.7 (Substitution)

A *substitution* is a partial mapping from variables to terms, with a finite domain. If the domain of the substitution σ is

$$dom(\sigma) = \{X_1, \ldots, X_n\}$$

we denote the substitution by $\{X_1 \mapsto t_1, \ldots, X_n \mapsto t_n\}$.

Substitutions are extended to terms and literals in the natural way: We apply a substitution σ to a term t or a literal l by simultaneously replacing each variable occurring in $dom(\sigma)$ by the corresponding term. The resulting term is denoted $t\sigma$.

Since substitutions are functions, *composition of substitutions* is simply functional composition. For example, $\sigma \cdot \rho$ denotes the composition of the substitutions σ and ρ.

Example 5.8

The application of the substitution

$$\sigma = \{X \mapsto g(Y), Y \mapsto a\}$$

to the term

$$f(f(X, g(a)), Y)$$

yields the term

$$f(f(g(Y), g(a)), a)$$

Note the simultaneous replacement of X and Y in the term above.

Since logic programs are first-order formulas, their meaning is precise. There is a *declarative interpretation* in which the semantics of a program is defined with respect to a mathematical model (the Herbrand universe). There is also a *procedural interpretation* of programs, which explains how the program is used in computations. The latter defines a logic-based computation model.

The computation associated with a logic program is defined through the use of SLD-resolution, a specific version of the Principle of Resolution. Using SLD-resolution, different alternatives to find a solution will be explored for a given goal in the context of a program. These alternatives will be represented as branches in a tree, called the *SLD-resolution tree* or simply SLD-tree. Some of the branches in the SLD-tree may not produce a solution; we need to traverse the whole tree (which can be infinite) in order to find all the solutions for a goal. The traversal of the tree can be done in different ways, and this will give us models of computation with different properties. Here we will consider a strategy for the traversal that explores each branch in depth, from left to right. Some branches may end with a failure (we will describe this notion below), and we will have to *backtrack* to the nearest point in the tree where there are still alternative branches to explore. We continue traversing the SLD-tree until all the alternatives are exhausted.

To illustrate the idea, let us look at a logic program defining the predicate **append** for lists. The empty list is denoted by the constant [], and a non-empty list is denoted as [X|L], where X represents the first element of the list (also called the *head*) and L is the rest of the list (also called the *tail* of the list). Note that [|] is a binary function symbol, a constructor that is used to build a list structure. We abbreviate [X|[]] as [X], [X|[Y|[]]] as [X,Y], and in general [X1,...,Xn] denotes a list of n elements.

Example 5.9

The predicate **append** is defined as a relation between three lists: the two lists we want to concatenate and their concatenation. More precisely, the atomic formula **append(S,T,U)** indicates that the result of appending the list T onto the end of the list S is the list U. We can define the predicate **append** by giving two program clauses (a fact and a rule):

```
append([],L,L).
append([X|L],Y,[X|Z]) :- append(L,Y,Z).
```

The predicate **append** defines a relation and can be used in different ways. For instance, a goal

```
:- append([0],[1,2],L).
```

will compute the answer substitution $\{L \mapsto [0,1,2]\}$, but with the *same* logic program and the goal

```
:- append([0],U,[0,1,2]).
```

we will obtain the solution $\{U \mapsto [1,2]\}$. In this case, the first and third arguments of the predicate are used as inputs and the second as output. All combinations are possible.

Answers to goals (i.e., substitutions mapping variables to values) will be automatically generated by the *unification algorithm*, which is part of the process of resolution. More precisely, to find the answer for a goal, we need to find in the program the clauses that can be applied; during this process, some equations between terms will be generated, and the unification algorithm will be called in order to solve these equations. If there is a solution, there is also one that is the most general solution in the sense that all the others can be derived from it. This is called the *most general unifier*. We will formally define unification problems and give a unification algorithm in the next section, but we can already give an example.

Example 5.10

To solve the query

    :- append([0],[1,2],U).

in the context of the logic program

    append([],L,L).
    append([X|L],Y,[X|Z]) :- append(L,Y,Z).

we will start by using the second program clause (the first one cannot be applied because in our goal the first list is not empty). The substitution

$$\{X \mapsto 0, \ L \mapsto [], \ Y \mapsto [1,2], \ U \mapsto [0|Z]\}$$

unifies the head of the second program clause with the query; that is, if we apply this substitution to the literals append([X|L],Y,[X|Z]) and append([0],[1,2],U) we obtain exactly the same result:

$$\text{append([0],[1,2],[0|Z]).}$$

Since the second clause in the program says that append([X|L],Y,[X|Z]) holds if append(L,Y,Z) holds, all that remains to be proved is that append([],[1,2],Z) holds for some Z.

Now we have an atom in which the first list is empty, and we have a fact append([],L,L) in the program. Applying the substitution

$$\{Z \mapsto [1,2]\}$$

to our atom, we obtain (an instance of) a fact.

Combining both substitutions we get

$$\{U \mapsto [0,1,2]\}$$

which solves the query. It is the most general answer substitution for the given goal, and the process by which we derived this solution is an example of an application of the Principle of Resolution.

Goals such as

```
:- append([0],[1,2],U)
:- append(X,[1,2],U)
:- append([1,2], U,[0])
```

can all be seen as questions to be answered using the definitions given in the program. The first one has only one solution:

$$\{U \mapsto [0,1,2]\}$$

The second has an infinite number of solutions, and the third one has none.

5.3 Computing with logic programs

In this section, we will describe how logic programs are executed, or in other words how computations are carried out in a model of computation where algorithms are expressed as logic programs. We have already mentioned in the previous section that the Principle of Resolution is the basis of this computation model. We will start by defining unification, a key step in the Principle of Resolution. Then we will define SLD-resolution, which uses a specific strategy to search for solutions to goals.

5.3.1 Unification

Although a process of unification was sketched by Herbrand in his thesis in the early 1930s, it was only in the 1960s, after Alan Robinson introduced the Principle of Resolution and gave an algorithm to unify terms, that logic programming became possible. Robinson's unification algorithm was the basis for the implementation of the programming language Prolog. The version of the unification algorithm that we present is based on the work of Martelli and

Montanari, where unification is described as a simplification process to solve equations between terms.

Definition 5.11 (Unifier)

A *unification problem* $\mathcal{U}$ is a set of equations between terms containing variables. We will use the notation

$$\{s_1 = t_1, \ldots, s_n = t_n\}$$

A solution to $\mathcal{U}$, also called a *unifier*, is a substitution σ (see Definition 5.7) such that when we apply σ to all the terms in the equations in $\mathcal{U}$ we obtain syntactical identities: For each equation $s_i = t_i$, the terms $s_i\sigma$ and $t_i\sigma$ coincide.

A unifier σ is said to be *most general* if any other unifier for the problem can be obtained as an instance of σ.

Although there may be many different substitutions that are most general unifiers, one can show that they are all equivalent modulo renaming of variables. In other words, the most general unifier is unique if we consider it modulo renamings. The algorithm of Martelli and Montanari finds the most general unifier for a unification problem if a solution exists; otherwise it fails, indicating that there are no solutions. To find the most general unifier for a unification problem, the algorithm simplifies (i.e., transforms) the set of equations until a substitution is generated. The simplification rules apply to sets of equations and produce new sets of equations or a failure.

Unification algorithm

Input: A finite set of equations between terms:

$$\{s_1 = t_1, \ldots, s_n = t_n\}$$

Output: A substitution that is the most general unifier (mgu) for these terms or failure.

Transformation rules: The rules that are given below transform a unification problem into a simpler one or produce a failure. Below, E denotes an arbitrary set of equations between terms.

(1) $f(s_1, \ldots, s_n) = f(t_1, \ldots, t_n), E \quad \rightarrow \quad s_1 = t_1, \ldots, s_n = t_n, E$

(2) $f(s_1, \ldots, s_n) = g(t_1, \ldots, t_m), E \quad \rightarrow \quad failure$

(3) $\qquad\qquad\qquad X = X, E \quad \rightarrow \quad E$

(4) $\qquad\qquad\qquad t = X, E \quad \rightarrow \quad X = t, E \qquad$ if t is not a variable

(5) $\qquad\qquad\qquad X = t, E \quad \rightarrow \quad X = t, E\{X \mapsto t\} \qquad$ if X is not in t and X occurs in E

(6) $\qquad\qquad\qquad X = t, E \quad \rightarrow \quad failure \qquad$ if x occurs in t and $x \neq t$

The unification algorithm applies the transformation rules in a non-deterministic way until no rule can be applied or a failure arises. Note that we are working with *sets* of equations, and therefore the order in which they appear in the unification problem is not important.

The test in case (6) is called *occur-check*; for example, $X = f(X)$ fails. This test is time-consuming, and for this reason in some systems it is not implemented.

If the algorithm finishes without a failure, we obtain a substitution, which is the *most general unifier* of the initial set of equations.

Note that rules (1) and (2) apply also to constants (i.e., 0-ary functions): In the first case, the equation is deleted, and in the second there is a failure.

Example 5.12

1. We start with $\{f(a, a) = f(X, a)\}$.

   a) Using rule (1), this problem is rewritten as $\{a = X, a = a\}$.

   b) Using rule (4), we get $\{X = a, a = a\}$.

   c) Using rule (1) again, we get $\{X = a\}$.

   Now no rule can be applied, and therefore the algorithm terminates with the most general unifier $\{X \mapsto a\}$.

2. In Example 5.10, we solved the unification problem

   $\{[X|L] = [0], Y = [1,2], [X|Z] = U\}$

Recall that [|] is a binary function symbol (a list constructor; its arguments are the head and the tail of the list, respectively). [0] is shorthand for [0|[]], and [] is a constant (the empty list).

We apply the unification algorithm, starting with the set of equations above.

a) Using rule (1) in the first equation, we get

   {X = 0, L = [], Y = [1,2], [X|Z] = U}

b) Using rule (5) and the first equation, we get

   {X = 0, L = [], Y = [1,2], [0|Z] = U}

c) Using rule (4) and the last equation, we get

   {X = 0, L = [], Y = [1,2], U = [0|Z]}

Then the algorithm stops. Therefore the most general unifier is

{X $\mapsto$ 0, L $\mapsto$ [],Y $\mapsto$ [1,2], U $\mapsto$ [0|Z]}

5.3.2 The Principle of Resolution

Resolution is based on *refutation*. In order to solve a query

:- $A_1, \ldots, A_n$

with respect to a set P of program clauses, resolution seeks to show that

$$P, \neg A_1, \ldots, \neg A_n$$

leads to a contradiction. That is, the negation of the literals in the goal is added to the program P; if a contradiction arises, then we know that P did entail the literals in the query.

Definition 5.13

A contradiction is obtained when a literal and its negation are stated at the same time.

For example, A, $\neg A$ is a contradiction. If a contradiction does not arise directly from the program and the goal, new clauses will be derived by resolution, and the process will continue until a contradiction arises (the search may continue forever). The derived clauses are called *resolvents*.

We will describe the generation of resolvents using a restriction of the Principle of Resolution called SLD-resolution; Prolog is based on SLD-resolution.

5.3.2.1 SLD-resolution. Let us consider first a simple case where in the query there is just one atom. If we have a goal

:- $p(u_1, \ldots, u_n)$.

and a program clause (we rename the variables in the clause if necessary so that all the variables are different from those in the goal)

$p(t_1, \ldots, t_n)$:- $S_1, \ldots, S_m$.

such that $p(t_1, \ldots, t_n)$ and $p(u_1, \ldots, u_n)$ are unifiable with mgu σ, then we obtain the resolvent

:- $S_1\sigma, \ldots, S_m\sigma$.

In the general case, the query may have several literals. Prolog's SLD-resolution generates a resolvent using the first literal in the goal.

Definition 5.14 (SLD-resolution)

If the query has several literals, for instance

:- $A_1, \ldots, A_k$.

the *resolvent* is computed between the *first* atom in the goal (A_1) and a (possibly renamed) program clause. If there is a program clause

A_1' :- $S_1, \ldots, S_m$.

such that A_1' and A_1 are unifiable with mgu σ, then we obtain a resolvent

:- $S_1\sigma, \ldots, S_m\sigma, A_2\sigma, \ldots, A_k\sigma$.

In other words, the resolvent is generated by replacing the first atom in the goal that unifies with the head of a clause by the body of the clause and applying the unifier to all the atoms in the new goal. Note that when we compute a resolvent using a fact (i.e., when $m = 0$), the atom disappears from the query. An empty resolvent indicates a contradiction, which we will denote by the symbol $\Diamond$.

We stress the fact that each resolution step computes a resolvent between the first atom of the last resolvent obtained and a clause in the program. This is why this particular form of resolution is called *SLD-resolution*.

The 'S' stands for *selection rule*: A fixed computation rule is applied in order to select a particular atom to resolve upon in the goal. Prolog always selects the *leftmost* literal in the goal.

The 'D' stands for *definite*: It indicates that all the program clauses are definite.

The 'L' stands for *linear*, indicating that each resolution step uses the most recent resolvent (to start with, it uses the given query) and a program clause. Prolog uses the clauses in the program *in the order they are written*.

Given a logic program and a query, the idea is to continue generating resolvents until an empty one (a contradiction) is generated. When an empty resolvent is generated, the composition of all the substitutions applied at each resolution step leading to the contradiction is computed. This is also a substitution (recall that substitutions are functions from terms to terms, and composition is simply functional composition; see Definition 5.7 for more details). The restriction of this substitution to the variables that occur in the initial goal is the *answer* to the initial query.

We represent each resolution step graphically as follows:

Query

$\mid mgu$

Resolvent

Since there might be several clauses in the program that can be used to generate a resolvent for a given query, we obtain a branching structure called an *SLD-resolution tree*.

Definition 5.15 (SLD-tree)

Every branch in the SLD-tree that leads to an empty resolvent produces an answer. All the branches that produce an answer are called *success branches*.

If a finite branch does not lead to an empty resolvent, it is a *failure*.

An SLD-resolution tree may have several success branches, failure branches, and also infinite branches that arise when we can continue to generate resolvents but never reach an empty one.

Example 5.16

Consider the program P

```
based(prolog,logic).
based(haskell,functions).
likes(max,logic).
likes(claire,functions).
likes(X,P) :- based(P,Y), likes(X,Y).
```

and the query

```
:- likes(Z,prolog).
```

Using the last clause and the mgu $\{X \mapsto Z, P \mapsto prolog\}$, we obtain the resolvent

```
:- based(prolog,Y), likes(Z,Y).
```

Now using the first clause and the mgu $\{Y \mapsto logic\}$, we obtain the new resolvent

```
:- likes(Z,logic).
```

Finally, since we can unify this atom with the fact `likes(max,logic)` using the substitution $\{Z \mapsto max\}$, we obtain an empty resolvent. This is therefore a success branch in the SLD-tree for the initial query.

The composition of the substitutions used in this branch is

$$\{X \mapsto max, P \mapsto prolog, Y \mapsto logic, Z \mapsto max\}$$

Therefore, the answer to the initial query is $\{Z \mapsto max\}$.

There are other branches in the SLD-tree for this query, but this is the only successful one. The SLD-resolution tree for this query is shown in Figure 5.1. Note that in the branch that leads to failure we again use the last clause of the program but rename its variables as `X'`, `P'`, `Y'` to avoid confusion with the previous use of this clause (see Definition 5.14).

Now consider the same program with an additional clause:

```
likes(claire,logic).
```

```
likes(Z,prolog)
```

$| \{X \mapsto Z, P \mapsto prolog\}$

```
based(prolog,Y), likes(Z,Y)
```

$| \{Y \mapsto logic\}$

```
likes(Z,logic).
```

$\{Z \mapsto max\} / \quad \backslash \{X' \mapsto Z, P' \mapsto logic\}$

$\diamondsuit \qquad$ `based(logic,Y'),likes(Z,Y')`
(Failure)

Figure 5.1 SLD-resolution tree for the query :- `likes(Z,prolog)`. using the program P.

The new program will be called P'. The SLD-resolution tree for the same query in the context of the program P' is shown in Figure 5.2.

```
likes(Z,prolog)
```

$| \{X \mapsto Z, P \mapsto prolog\}$

```
based(prolog,Y), likes(Z,Y)
```

$| \{Y \mapsto logic\}$

```
likes(Z,logic).
```

$\{Z \mapsto max\}/ \{Z \mapsto claire\}| \qquad \backslash$

$\diamondsuit \qquad\qquad \diamondsuit \qquad$ `based(logic,Y'),likes(Z,Y')`
(Failure)

Figure 5.2 SLD-tree for :- `likes(Z,prolog)`. using the program P'.

Finally, with the same program and a query

:- `likes(Z,painting)`.

the SLD-tree is

$$\texttt{likes(Z,painting)}$$

$$\mid \{\texttt{X} \mapsto \texttt{Z},\ \texttt{P} \mapsto \texttt{painting}\}$$

$$\texttt{based(painting,Y), likes(Z,Y)}$$
$$(\textit{Failure})$$

5.4 Prolog and the logic programming paradigm

We have seen how logic formulas can be used to express knowledge and describe problems and how we can compute solutions to a problem using resolution as the inference rule. In this section, we discuss the logic programming paradigm.

If we analyse the approaches to programming discussed in the previous chapters (imperative and functional), we can single out one major difference: Functional programs are concerned with *what* needs to be computed, whereas imperative programs indicate *how* to compute it. Functional languages are *declarative*. *Logic programming languages* also belong to the family of declarative languages. Roughly speaking, programs in logic programming languages specify a problem, and the execution of a program is a process of proof searching during which solutions for the problem will be generated. Since programs are just descriptions of problems, this is a knowledge-based programming style that has many applications in artificial intelligence (for example, to build expert systems).

The language of logic is a very powerful one. The same formalism can be used to specify a problem, write a program, and prove properties of the program. The same program can be used in many different ways. Based on this idea, several programming languages have been developed that differ in the kind of logic that is used for the description of the problem and the method employed to find proofs. The most well-known logic programming language is *Prolog*, which is based on first-order predicate calculus and uses the Principle of Resolution. Actually, first-order logic and the Principle of Resolution are too general to be used directly as a model of computation, but in the 1970s Robert Kowalski, Alain Colmerauer, and Philippe Roussel defined and implemented a suitable restriction based on the clausal fragment of classical first-order logic, as described in the previous sections. Their work resulted in the first version of Prolog.

Prolog builds the SLD-tree for a given query using the clauses in the program in the order in which they occur, in a depth-first manner: The leftmost branch in the SLD-tree is generated first. If this branch is infinite, Prolog will fail to find an answer even if there are other successful branches. For this reason, the order of the clauses in a Prolog program is very important.

If during the traversal of the tree Prolog arrives at a failure leaf, it will go back (towards the root of the tree) to explore the remaining branches. This process is called *backtracking*.

We could summarise Prolog's computations as SLD-resolution with a depth-first search strategy and automatic backtracking.

Example 5.17

Consider the program P defining the predicate append:

```
append([],L,L).
append([X|L],Y,[X|Z]) :- append(L,Y,Z).
```

The goal

```
:- append(X,[1,2],U).
```

produces the answer $\{X \mapsto [], U \mapsto [1, 2]\}$, but if we change the order of the clauses in the program, the same goal leads to an infinite computation. In this case, there is no answer for the query, and eventually the interpreter will give an error message (out of memory space because the leftmost branch of the SLD-tree that Prolog is trying to build is infinite).

SLD-resolution has interesting computational properties:

1. It is refutation-complete: Given a Prolog program and a goal, if a contradiction can be derived, then SLD-resolution will eventually generate an empty resolvent.

2. It is independent of the computation rule: If there is an answer for a goal, SLD-resolution will find it whichever selection rule is employed for choosing the literals resolved upon.

However, the particular tree traversal strategy that Prolog uses is not complete. In the example above, we see that if we change the order of the clauses in the program, Prolog fails to find an answer, even if an empty resolvent can be generated by SLD-resolution. The problem is that this empty resolvent will be generated in a branch of the SLD-tree that Prolog does not build.

There is an easy way to obtain a refutation-complete implementation of SLD-resolution: using a breadth-first search instead of a depth-first search. However, there is a price to pay. A breadth-first search strategy will in general take more time to find the first answer. For this reason, this strategy is not used in practice.

Nowadays, several versions of Prolog exist. The basic framework has been enriched to make it more efficient and easier to use. Extensions include primitive data types such as integers and real numbers, advanced optimisation techniques, file-handling facilities, graphical interfaces, control mechanisms, and others. Some of these features are non-declarative, and often programs that use them are called *impure* because, to achieve efficiency in the program, the problem description is mixed with implementation details (i.e., the *what* and the *how* are mixed). Constraint logic programming languages, which were developed from Prolog, achieve efficiency by incorporating optimised proof search methods for specific domains.

5.5 Further reading

We refer the reader to [23] for more examples of logic programs. Robinson's article [43] introduces the Principle of Resolution. More information on the unification algorithm presented in this chapter can be found in Martelli and Montanari's article [31]. The book [7] provides an introduction to logic programming, and [44] is a reference document for Prolog.

5.6 Exercises

1. Assuming that A, B, C are atoms, which of the following clauses are Horn clauses?

   a) $\neg A$

   b) $A \vee B \vee \neg C$

   c) $A \vee \neg A$

   d) A

2. Numbers and arithmetic operations are predefined in Prolog. Assume we define the predicate **mean** using the clause

   ```
   mean(A,B,C) :- C is (A+B)/2.
   ```

What are the answers to the following goals?

`:- mean(2,4,X).`

`:- mean(2,4,6).`

3. Show that for the problem `f(X) = f(Y)` both $\{X \mapsto Y\}$ and $\{Y \mapsto X\}$ are most general solutions. Can you find a different substitution that is also a most general unifier for these terms?

4. Give the most general unifier (if it exists) of the following atoms (recall that `[1,2]` is short for the list `[1|[2|[]]]`):

   a) `append([1,2],X,U)`, `append([Y|L],Z,[Y|R])`

   b) `append([1,2],X,[0,1])`, `append([Y|L],Z,[Y|R])`

   c) `append([],X,[0,1])`, `append([Y|L],Z,[Y|R])`

   d) `append([],X,[0])`, `append([],[X|L],[Y])`

5. Lists are predefined in Prolog; in particular, the predicate `append` is predefined, but in this exercise we will define a new append:

   `myappend([],Y,Y).`

   `myappend([H|T],Y,[H|U]) :- myappend(T,Y,U).`

   What are the answers to the following goals?

   `:- myappend([1,2],[3,4,5],[1,2,3,4,5]).`

   `:- myappend([1,2],[3,4,5],[1,2]).`

   `:- myappend([1,2],[3,4,5],X).`

   `:- myappend([1,2],X,[1,2,3,4,5]).`

   `:- myappend(X,[3,4,5],[1,2,3,4,5]).`

   `:- myappend(X,Y,[1,2,3,4,5]).`

   `:- myappend(X,Y,Z).`

   Explain the answers.

6. Show that the resolvent of the clauses

   `P :-` $A_1, \ldots, A_n$

   and

:- $Q_1, \ldots, Q_m$

is also a Horn clause.

7. Consider the program

```
nat(s(X)) :- nat(X).

nat(0).
```

and the query

```
:- nat(Y).
```

a) Describe the complete SLD-resolution tree for this query.

b) Explain why Prolog will not find an answer for this query.

c) Change the program so that Prolog can find an answer.

8. Write a logic program defining a binary predicate **member** such that member(a,l) is true if the element **a** is in the list **l**.

What are the answers to the following queries? Draw the SLD-resolution tree for each one.

a) :- member(1,[2,1,3]).

b) :- member(1,[2,3,4]).

c) :- member(1,[]).

9. What is the purpose of the *occur-check* in the unification algorithm?

10. Write a logic program for sorting a list of numbers (in ascending order) using the insertion sort algorithm.

For this, you will need to define:

– a predicate **sort** such that sort(L,L') holds if L' is a list containing the same elements as L but in ascending order; and

– a predicate **insertion** such that insertion(X,L,L') holds if X is a number, L is a sorted list (in ascending order), and L' is the result of inserting X in the corresponding place in the list L.

11. Consider the following program and queries:

Program:

```
even(0).

even(s(s(X))) :- even(X).
```

```
odd(s(0)).
```

```
odd(X) :- even(s(X)).
```

Queries:

```
:- odd(s(s(0))).
```

```
:- odd(s(0)).
```

Write an SLD-resolution tree for each query.

We now replace the fourth clause of the program by

```
odd(X) :- greater(X,s(0)), even(s(X)).
```

Write the clauses defining the predicate **greater** such that **greater(m,n)** holds when the number **m** is greater than **n**.

Give the SLD-tree for the query

```
:-odd(s(0)).
```

with the modified program.

12. A graph is a set $V = \{a, b, c, \ldots\}$ of vertices and a set $E \subseteq V \times V$ of edges. We use the binary predicate **edge** to represent the edges: **edge(a,b)** means that there is an edge from **a** to **b**. In a directed graph, the edges have a direction, so **edge(a,b)** is different from **edge(b,a)**. We say that there is a *path* from a to b in a graph if there is a sequence of one or more edges that allows us to go from a to b.

    a) Write a logic program defining the predicate **path**.

    b) Write a query to compute all the directed paths starting from **a** in the graph.

    c) Write a query to compute all the directed paths in the graph.

Part II

Modern Models of Computation

6

Computing with Objects

Turing machines and the λ-calculus are two examples of universal (i.e., Turing-complete) models of computation. We will now describe another universal model, based on the use of objects, with method invocation and update as main operations.

Many modern programming languages are based on the object model: Java, Eiffel, C++, Smalltalk, Self, OCaml, OHaskell, etc. In defining an object-based model of computation, we will try to encapsulate the essential features of object-oriented programming languages. These are:

– the ability to create objects, which are collections of fields and methods;

– the ability to use a method belonging to an object — this is usually called *method invocation*, but sometimes the terminology "message passing" is used;

– the ability to modify a method in an object — this is usually called *method update* or *method override*.

An object calculus is the analogue of the λ-calculus for objects rather than functions. The object calculus that we will describe was introduced by Martín Abadi and Luca Cardelli in the 1990s. It has primitives to define methods (and fields as a particular case), to call methods that have already been defined, and to update them. It can be seen as a minimal object-oriented programming language or as the kernel of an object-oriented language. We will see that the calculus of objects has the same computation power as the λ-calculus.

In the description of the object calculus in this chapter, we will follow the same pattern as for the λ-calculus. We present first the syntax of the object calculus, then the reduction rules we will use to compute with objects, and finally we will discuss the properties of the calculus and its applications to the design of object-oriented programming languages.

6.1 Object calculus: Syntax

We start by defining the syntax of the terms that we will use to represent objects and operations on them.

Objects will be represented as collections of methods, each method having a different label (its name) and body (the method's definition). The body of a method can refer to the whole object where the method is defined; in other words, objects can contain self-references. This is done by using a distinguished variable, called *self* or *this* in object-oriented programming languages. In the object calculus, we will simply use a bound variable. Thus a method will have the form $l = \varsigma(x)b$, where l is the name of the method, and the occurrences of x in b will represent the object where the method is defined. We say that the variable x is *bound* in $\varsigma(x)b$, and ς is a binder (like λ in the λ-calculus). Because of the use of this symbol as a binder, the object calculus is sometimes called ς-calculus.

Methods that do not use a self-reference in their definition are called *fields*; in other words, a field is a method of the form $l = \varsigma(x)b$, where b does not contain any occurrence of x. In this case, it can simply be written $l = b$.

We write objects by listing their methods between square brackets:

$$[l_1 = \varsigma(x_1)b_1, \ldots, l_n = \varsigma(x_n)b_n]$$

We will sometimes use the notation $[l_i = \varsigma(x_i)b_i^{i \in 1 \ldots n}]$ as an abbreviation. Note that the order in which we write the methods in an object is not important (objects are *sets* of methods).

We assume that there is an infinite, countable set $\mathcal{X}$ of variables $x, y, z, \ldots, x_1, x_2, \ldots$, and an infinite, countable set $\mathcal{L}$ of labels $l_1, \ldots, l_n, \ldots$, such that $\mathcal{X}$ and $\mathcal{L}$ are disjoint. The language of terms in the ς-calculus is defined by induction, with variables as a base case, as described below.

Definition 6.1

The set $\mathcal{O}$ of terms is the smallest set that contains

– all the variables in $\mathcal{X}$;

– objects of the form $[l_i = \varsigma(x_i)b_i^{i \in 1 \ldots n}]$, where $l_i \in \mathcal{L}$, $x_i \in \mathcal{X}$, and $b_i \in \mathcal{O}$, for all $i \in \{1, \ldots, n\}$;

– method invocations $a.l$, where $a \in \mathcal{O}$ and $l \in \mathcal{L}$; and

– method updates $a.l \Leftarrow \varsigma(x)b$, where $a, b \in \mathcal{O}$, $l \in \mathcal{L}$, $x \in \mathcal{X}$.

An invocation $a.l$ denotes a call to the method with label l in the object a. Update operations will be used to modify method definitions (or fields as a particular case). For instance, $o.l \Leftarrow \varsigma(x)b$ will be used to replace (only) the method l in o with $\varsigma(x)b$. In the case of an update of a field, we will simply write $a.l := b$.

Since ς is a binder, we have an associated notion of free and bound variables. Any occurrence of a variable x in b is *bound* in the term $\varsigma(x)b$. Occurrences of variables that are not in the scope of a binder are free. The sets of free and bound variables of a term can be computed using the functions defined below.

Definition 6.2 (Free and bound variables)

The set of free variables of o will be denoted by $FV(o)$. This set can be computed as follows:

$$
\begin{aligned}
FV(x) &= \{x\} \\
FV(\varsigma(x)b) &= FV(b) - \{x\} \\
FV([l_i = \varsigma(x_i)b_i^{i \in 1 \ldots n}]) &= \bigcup^{i \in 1 \ldots n} FV(\varsigma(x_i)b_i) \\
FV(a.l) &= FV(a) \\
FV(a.l \Leftarrow \varsigma(x)b) &= FV(a) \cup FV(\varsigma(x)b)
\end{aligned}
$$

A term a is closed if it has no free variables; that is, $FV(a) = \emptyset$. The set of bound variables of o is also defined by induction:

$$
\begin{aligned}
BV(x) &= \emptyset \\
BV(\varsigma(x)b) &= BV(b) \cup \{x\} \\
BV([l_i = \varsigma(x_i)b_i^{i \in 1 \ldots n}]) &= \{x_1, \ldots, x_n\} \cup \bigcup^{i \in 1 \ldots n} BV(b_i) \\
BV(a.l) &= BV(a) \\
BV(a.l \Leftarrow \varsigma(x)b) &= BV(a) \cup BV(\varsigma(x)b)
\end{aligned}
$$

As in the λ-calculus, terms represent α-equivalence classes: Two terms that can be made equal by renaming their bound variables are considered equivalent. Many of these ideas will become clearer after we give the computation rules that define the dynamics of the calculus in the next section.

6.2 Reduction rules

There are two computation rules in the ς-calculus: The *invocation rule* describes the behaviour of a method invocation, and the *update rule* describes the effect of a method update. Object-oriented computation is described as a sequence of reduction steps using these rules; in other words, a computation is a sequence of method invocations and updates.

Consider an object $o = [l_i = \varsigma(x_i)b_i^{i \in 1 \dots n}]$. Intuitively, the invocation of the method l_j in o should trigger the evaluation of the body of this method (i.e., b_j). Since b_j may contain self-references (to the object o), before evaluating b_j all occurrences of x_j in b_j must be replaced by the object o. More precisely, the invocation of the method l_j in o triggers the evaluation of $b_j\{x_j \mapsto o\}$, where we use the notation $\{x_j \mapsto o\}$ to represent the substitution of x_j by o. This is the essence of the invocation rule. The update rule simply replaces a method with a new definition.

$$
\begin{array}{lll}
(invocation) & o.l_j & \longrightarrow \quad b_j\{x_j \mapsto o\} \\
(update) & o.l_j \Leftarrow \varsigma(y)b & \longrightarrow \quad [l_j = \varsigma(y)b, l_i = \varsigma(x_i)b_i^{i \in (1 \dots n) - j}]
\end{array}
$$

Substitution must be performed with care in the presence of bound variables. The notion of substitution used in the invocation rule is the same *capture-avoiding* notion of substitution that we defined for the λ-calculus in Chapter 3. We recall it below.

In both rules above, we assume $j \in 1 \dots n$. We now give a simple example.

Example 6.3

Consider an object o with only one method, called l, whose body is just a self-reference. In the ς-calculus, this object is defined by the term

$$o = [l = \varsigma(x)x]$$

Then, using the invocation rule, $o.l \longrightarrow o$.

As usual, we denote a sequence of reduction steps from t to u by $t \longrightarrow^* u$.

We define below the operation of substitution, taking into account the fact that terms are defined modulo α-equivalence: In substituting under a binder, we must avoid the capture of free variables.

Definition 6.4 (Substitution)

The substitution of x by c in a term o, written $o\{x \mapsto c\}$, is defined as follows:

$$
\begin{aligned}
x\{x \mapsto c\} &= c \\
y\{x \mapsto c\} &= y \\
(\varsigma(y)b)\{x \mapsto c\} &= \varsigma(y')(b\{y \mapsto y'\}\{x \mapsto c\}) \quad (y' \text{ fresh}) \\
([l_i = \varsigma(x_i)b_i^{i \in 1 \ldots n}])\{x \mapsto c\} &= [l_i = (\varsigma(x_i)b_i)\{x \mapsto c\}^{i \in 1 \ldots n}] \\
(a.l)\{x \mapsto c\} &= a\{x \mapsto c\}.l \\
(a.l \Leftarrow \varsigma(y)b)\{x \mapsto c\} &= (a\{x \mapsto c\}).l \Leftarrow (\varsigma(y)b)\{x \mapsto c\}
\end{aligned}
$$

Note that in the third case above, when we apply the substitution $\{x \mapsto c\}$ to $\varsigma(y)b$, the variable y is renamed to a fresh variable y' to ensure that there are no clashes with the variables in c.

Some examples of terms and computations in the object calculus follow.

Example 6.5

1. *Empty object:* It is possible to define an empty object, with no methods or fields, by writing [ ]. The object $o = [empty = [\,]]$ has just one field, and $o.empty \longrightarrow [\,]$.

2. *Self:* It is also possible to define an object with one method that returns the object itself, as shown in Example 6.3. If $o = [l = \varsigma(x)x]$, then $o.l \longrightarrow o$. In some object-oriented programming languages, this can be achieved by returning 'self' or 'this'.

3. *Non-termination:* Due to the possibility of defining recursive methods (that is, methods that invoke themselves), objects in this calculus may generate infinite computation sequences. For instance, if we define $o = [l = \varsigma(x)x.l]$, then the method invocation $o.l$ produces a non-terminating computation sequence:
$$
o.l \longrightarrow x.l\{x \mapsto o\} = o.l \longrightarrow \cdots
$$

The reduction relation generated by the invocation and update rules is confluent.

Property 6.6 (Confluence)

The ς-calculus is confluent: If $a \longrightarrow^* b$ and also $a \longrightarrow^* c$, then there is some d such that $b \longrightarrow^* d$ and $c \longrightarrow^* d$.

A term is in normal form if it is irreducible. Normal forms can be seen as results; when a program is evaluated, it produces a normal form or an infinite computation.

The confluence property implies the unicity of normal forms. Although some terms may not produce a result, if a program gives a result, then this result is uniquely determined.

6.3 Computation power

We mentioned at the beginning of the chapter that the object calculus is Turing complete. This can be proved by defining an encoding of the λ-calculus into the object calculus. Below we show an encoding, defined by Abadi and Cardelli, that is based on the idea that a function can be represented as an object with a field arg to store the function's argument and a field val that defines the function itself. Formally, the encoding is defined inductively. The idea is to give, for each class of λ-term, the corresponding ς-term. For this, we define a transformation function from λ-terms to ς-terms and show that the translated terms have the same behaviour. For the sake of uniformity, in this chapter we write λ-abstractions as $\lambda(n)t$ instead of $\lambda n.t$.

Definition 6.7

Let $\mathcal{T} : \lambda \to \varsigma$ be a function from λ-terms to ς-terms defined as follows:

$$\mathcal{T}(x) = x$$
$$\mathcal{T}(\lambda x.M) = [arg = \varsigma(x)x.arg, val = \varsigma(x)\mathcal{T}(M)\{x \mapsto x.arg\}]$$
$$\mathcal{T}(MN) = (\mathcal{T}(M).arg := \mathcal{T}(N)).val$$

According to the function $\mathcal{T}$, the encoding of a λ-abstraction is an object, where the body of the λ-abstraction is stored in the method val and any reference to its argument is replaced by a call to the method arg. Then, the encoding of an application simply stores the actual argument in the field arg and calls val.

To see that this encoding actually works, we need to show that the reductions out of a λ-term can be simulated by reductions on the ς-term obtained by the encoding. More precisely, we need to show that if $t \longrightarrow u$ in the λ-calculus, then $\mathcal{T}(t) \longrightarrow^* \mathcal{T}(u)$ in the ς-calculus. For this it is sufficient to show that

$$\mathcal{T}((\lambda x.M)N) \to^* \mathcal{T}(M\{x \mapsto N\}) = \mathcal{T}(M)\{x \mapsto \mathcal{T}(N)\}$$

which we can do as follows:

$$
\begin{aligned}
\mathcal{T}((\lambda x.M)N) &= (\mathcal{T}(\lambda x.M).arg := \mathcal{T}(N)).val \\
&= [arg = \mathcal{T}(N), val = \varsigma(x)\mathcal{T}(M)\{x \mapsto x.arg\}].val
\end{aligned}
$$

Let o be the object $[arg = \mathcal{T}(N), val = \varsigma(x)\mathcal{T}(M)\{x \mapsto x.arg\}]$. Then we can write $\mathcal{T}((\lambda x.M)N) = o.val$, and we have the following reduction steps:

$$
\begin{aligned}
o.val \quad &\longrightarrow \quad (\mathcal{T}(M)\{x \mapsto x.arg\})\{x \mapsto o\} \\
&= \quad \mathcal{T}(M)\{x \mapsto o.arg\} \\
&\longrightarrow^* \quad \mathcal{T}(M)\{x \mapsto \mathcal{T}(N)\}
\end{aligned}
$$

Although we did not include numbers or other data structures in the syntax of the ς-calculus, it should be clear that data structures can be encoded in this calculus. For instance, this can be done via an encoding into the λ-calculus, as shown in Chapter 3, which can itself be encoded in the ς-calculus as shown above. In what follows, we freely use numbers in examples.

6.4 Object-oriented programming

The object-oriented paradigm is one of the most popular in industry. There are two different flavours of object-oriented languages in use:

— *Class-based object-oriented languages:* These are the most widespread and include languages such as C++, Java, and Smalltalk. In class-based languages, there is a global hierarchy of object generators, called classes, organised by the inheritance relation. Every object is generated by a single class, and therefore the partial order between classes induces a categorisation and a partial order on objects.

— *Prototype-based object-oriented languages:* In these languages, objects can be defined directly, without first defining a class. There is a cloning operation that can be used to create additional copies of objects (i.e., objects are seen as *prototypes* that can be cloned). Examples of prototype-based languages are Self and Javascript. These languages, although less popular than class-based ones, present remarkable features in terms of flexibility, expressiveness, and conceptual simplicity.

The object calculus is classified as prototype-based since there is no primitive notion of class in the calculus. However, classes can be encoded in prototype-based calculi. Before showing the encoding, let us give some simple examples that relate the ς-calculus to class-based languages in the style of Java.

Consider the following program defining the class Empty:

```
class Empty {
}
```

```
class Test {
    public static void main(String[] args){
        Empty o = new Empty();
    }
}
```

Objects in the class `Empty` do not contain any fields or methods. The object o created with the command **new Empty()** corresponds to the object [ ] in the ς-calculus.

Consider now the object

$$o = [l = 3]$$

in the ς-calculus, and the new object obtained by evaluating the expression

$$o.l \Leftarrow 4$$

which updates the value of the field l. The same effect can be obtained by defining the following classes in Java:

```
class Number {
    int l = 3;
}
```

```
class Test {
    public static void main(String[] args){
        Number o = new Number();
        o.l = 4;
    }
}
```

The previous examples illustrate the creation of simple objects via the definition of classes and the definition of the same objects in a direct way in the ς-calculus. We can use this technique to simulate classes in the object calculus. Since there is no primitive notion of class in the object calculus, we will use objects to define classes. More precisely, a *class* will be an object with

– a method *new* for creating new objects and

– all the methods needed in the objects generated from the class.

For instance, to generate an object

$$o = [l_i = \varsigma(x_i)b_i^{i\in 1...n}]$$

we will use the class

$$c = [new = \varsigma(z)[l_i = \varsigma(x)z.l_i(x)^{i\in 1...n}], l_j = \lambda(x_j)b_j^{j\in 1...n}]$$

It is easy to see that $c.new = o$ since $c.new \longrightarrow [l_i = \varsigma(x)c.l_i(x)^{i\in 1...n}]$, and $c.l_i(x) = b_i$.

We call the method new a $generator$. Each field l_i is called a premethod.

As the attentive reader might have noticed, in this encoding of classes we have also used the λ-calculus: We have defined the methods l_j in the class c as λ-abstractions (i.e., functions) with formal argument x_j and body b_j. However, it is also possible to encode classes using just the object calculus since we have already shown that the λ-calculus can be encoded in the ς-calculus.

As this encoding shows, it is convenient to have access to both object primitives and functions in the same calculus. We will define functional extensions of the object calculus below.

6.5 Combining objects and functions

Although object-oriented languages are popular, languages that are based solely on objects deprive users of a certain number of useful programming techniques available in other paradigms (e.g., pattern matching on data, typical of modern functional programming languages). Ideally, we would like a programming language to offer the best features of each of the programming paradigms. However, combining object-oriented and functional programming styles in a single multiparadigm language is not an easy task. The problem is finding a uniform way of integrating both styles rather than glueing together a functional and an object-oriented language. Several solutions have been proposed; for instance, the programming languages OCaml, OHaskell, and Scala smoothly integrate features of object-oriented languages and functional languages. Their underlying model of computation can be explained by extending the ς-calculus to include other features, such as

- basic data types (e.g., numbers, Booleans),

- the λ-calculus, and

- more general reduction systems.

There are several motivations for using such combinations. For instance, it is generally more efficient to add "built-in" data structures rather than define them in the basic calculus (numbers especially). Also, other calculi may provide a more natural representation for certain features; typically, an input-output behaviour is more naturally captured as a function, and functions are more naturally represented using the λ-calculus.

The addition of features such as numbers and functions allows the programmer to define in a concise way systems that would require heavy encodings in the ς-calculus. However, the addition of these features does not offer any additional computation power. We have already seen that we can encode the λ-calculus in the ς-calculus, and we can also encode numbers in these calculi. Thus we can always replace the new features with the corresponding simulation in the pure object calculus.

It is also possible to model imperative features in the object calculus; for instance, memory locations (which can be directly manipulated in an imperative language) can also be initialised and updated using the object calculus, as the following example shows.

Example 6.8

We can model a memory cell in the ς-calculus by using an object with a field to store a value and a method *set* to change this value. The object *loc* defined below represents a memory location storing the value 0.

$$loc = [value = 0, set = \varsigma(x)\lambda(n)x.value := n]$$

In this example, the field *value* contains a number, and the method *set* allows us to change this number.

The method invocation *loc.value* can be used to retrieve the value stored at the location. Note that the method *set* is defined using a function (represented by a λ-abstraction) that takes as its argument the new value n to be stored at the location.

Below we show a reduction sequence for the term $loc.set(2)$:

$$
\begin{aligned}
loc.set(2) \quad &\longrightarrow \quad (\lambda(n)[value = 0, set = \varsigma(x)\lambda(n)x.value := n].value := n)2 \\
&\longrightarrow \quad [value = 0, set = \varsigma(x)\lambda(n)x.value := n].value := 2 \\
&\longrightarrow \quad [value = 2, set = \varsigma(x)\lambda(n)x.value := n]
\end{aligned}
$$

Thus $loc.set(2).value \longrightarrow^* 2$.

Functional and object-oriented computations fit naturally in the example above. The functional part in this example models the input of the value (in this case the number 2), and the object-oriented part models the update of the memory location with the input value.

We give below another example that shows the combined use of functions and objects to model the behaviour of a pocket calculator.

Example 6.9 (Calculator)

The calculator will be represented by an object *calc*, with an accumulator, represented by the field *acc*, and methods representing the arithmetic operations addition, subtraction, etc. The method *equals* behaves like the key $=$ in a pocket calculator.

$$
\begin{aligned}
calc \quad = \quad & [arg = 0.0, \\
& acc = 0.0, \\
& enter = \varsigma(s)\lambda(n)s.arg := n, \\
& add = \varsigma(s)(s.acc := s.equals).equals \Leftarrow \varsigma(s')s'.acc + s'.arg, \\
& sub = \varsigma(s)(s.acc := s.equals).equals \Leftarrow \varsigma(s')s'.acc - s'.arg, \\
& \quad \cdots \\
& equals = \varsigma(s)s.arg]
\end{aligned}
$$

For example, the term $calc.enter(5.0).equals$ reduces to the value 5.0, and $calc.enter(5.0).sub.enter(3.5).equals$ reduces to 1.5.

In the example above, we have used an extension of the ς-calculus that includes numbers and basic functions to operate on them. The extension does not increase the computation power of the calculus but makes it easier to use. A more radical approach consists of adding general rewrite rules of the form

$$ l \to r $$

where l and r are terms. A rewrite rule can be thought of as an oriented equality, or a simplification step that can be used to compute the value of an expression. For example, $x + 0 \to x$ is a rewrite rule with the intended meaning that to compute the result of $x + 0$ for any arbitrary expression x we just need to compute the value of x.

An extension of this kind, with arbitrary rewrite rules, can change the computation properties of the calculus since it is not the case that all rewrite rules can be encoded in the ς-calculus. The reason is simply that the addition of arbitrary reduction rules can break the confluence of the system. Moreover, even if we restrict the extension to sets of confluent rules, the resulting system may be non-confluent, as the following example shows.

Consider the rewrite system

$$ f\ x\ x \longrightarrow 0 $$
$$ f\ x\ S(x) \longrightarrow 1 $$

This system is confluent, but the combination of the ς-calculus with such rules leads to a non-confluent system. Take $o = [l = \varsigma(x)S(x.l)]$, and examine the possible results of $f\ o.l\ o.l$. Using the first rule,

$$ f\ o.l\ o.l \to 0 $$

Using the invocation rule, $o.l \longrightarrow S(o.l)$, and therefore

$$f\ o.l\ o.l \to f\ o.l\ S(o.l) \to 1$$

However, if we extend the ς-calculus using only left-linear rules (that is, rules such that on the left-hand side each variable occurs at most once), then the extended calculus is confluent. In particular, all the extensions mentioned above (ς-calculus combined with numbers and arithmetic operations, ς-calculus combined with λ-calculus, etc.) fall into this class and are therefore confluent.

6.6 Further reading

For more details on object calculi, we refer the reader to Abadi and Cardelli's book [1]. The class-based object-oriented programming languages C++, Java, and Smalltalk are described in [48], [20], and [25], respectively. For further information about prototype languages, see the descriptions of Self [52] and Javascript [13]. For more details on languages combining object-oriented and functional features, see the descriptions of OCaml [30] and Scala [38]. Further information on combinations of object calculi and rewrite rules can be found in [9].

6.7 Exercises

1. What is the fundamental difference between a method defined by $l = \varsigma(x)b$ in an object o and a function with argument x defined by the λ-term $\lambda(x)b$?

2. Describe at least two different ways to encode numbers in the object calculus.

3. Add a method *get* in the object *loc* defined in Example 6.8 to represent a memory location, so that the field *value* is accessed by *get*.

4. In a calculus that combines objects, functions, numbers, and arithmetic functions, we have defined the following object:

$$\begin{aligned}
loc \ \ = \ \ &[value = 0, \\
&set = \varsigma(x)\lambda(n)x.value := n, \\
&incr = \varsigma(x)x.value := x.value + 1]
\end{aligned}$$

a) Describe in your own words the behaviour of the methods *set* and *incr*.

b) Evaluate the terms (and show the reduction steps)

    i. *loc.set*(1).*set*(3).*value*

    ii. *loc.incr.value*

where *loc* is the object defined above.

5. Show the reduction sequences for the following terms using the definition of the calculator in Example 6.9:

$$calc.enter(5.0).equals$$
$$calc.enter(5.0).sub.enter(3.5).equals$$
$$calc.enter(5.0).add.add.equals$$

6. Recall the translation function $\mathcal{T}$ from the λ-calculus to the ς-calculus defined in this chapter:

$$\mathcal{T}(x) = x$$
$$\mathcal{T}(\lambda x.M) = [arg = \varsigma(x)x.arg, val = \varsigma(x)\mathcal{T}(M)\{x \mapsto x.arg\}]$$
$$\mathcal{T}(MN) = (\mathcal{T}(M).arg := \mathcal{T}(N)).val$$

a) Using this definition, write down the ς-terms obtained by the following translations:

    i. $\mathcal{T}(\lambda x.x)$

    ii. $\mathcal{T}(\lambda xy.x)$

    iii. $\mathcal{T}(\lambda y.(\lambda x.x)y)$

    iv. $\mathcal{T}((\lambda x.x)(\lambda y.y))$

b) Reduce $\mathcal{T}((\lambda x.x)(\lambda y.y))$ to normal form using the reduction rules of the ς-calculus.

c) What are the advantages and disadvantages of a computation model that combines the ς-calculus and additional rewriting rules? Compare it with the pure ς-calculus.

7. Indicate whether each of the following statements about the ς-calculus is true or false and why.

a) The ς-calculus is confluent; therefore each expression has at most one normal form in this calculus.

b) The ς-calculus does not have an operation to add methods to an object; therefore it is not a Turing-complete model of computation.

7

Interaction-Based Models of Computation

In this chapter, we study interaction nets, a model of computation that can be seen as a representative of a class of models based on the notion of "computation as interaction". Interaction nets are a *graphical* model of computation devised by Yves Lafont in 1990 as a generalisation of the proof structures of linear logic. It can be seen as an abstract formalism, used to define algorithms and analyse their cost, or as a low-level language into which other programming languages can be compiled. This is fruitful because interaction nets can be implemented with reasonable efficiency.

An interaction net system is specified by a set of *agents* and a set of *interaction rules*. One can think of agents as logical symbols (connectives) and interaction rules as a specification of their meaning. There is also an analogy with electric circuits, where the agents are seen as gates and the edges as wires connecting the gates. Or we can simply think of the agents as computation entities, with interaction rules specifying their behaviour.

In the following sections, we give an overview of the interaction paradigm, give examples of uses of interaction nets to express algorithms, and also show how other computation models can be encoded in interaction nets.

7.1 The paradigm of interaction

Interaction net systems are specified by giving a set Σ of symbols used to build nets and a set $\mathcal{R}$ of rewrite rules, called *interaction rules*, that must satisfy the set of conditions given below. Each symbol $\alpha \in \Sigma$ has an associated (fixed) *arity*, a natural number. We assume that the function $\mathsf{ar} : \Sigma \to \mathsf{Nat}$ provides the arity of each symbol in Σ.

Definition 7.1 (Net)

A net N built on Σ is a graph (not necessarily connected) where nodes are labelled by symbols in Σ. A labelled node is called an *agent*, and an edge between two agents is called a *wire*, so nets are graphs built out of agents and wires.

The points of attachment of wires are called *ports*. If the arity of α is n, then a node labelled with α must have $n + 1$ ports: a distinguished one called the *principal port*, depicted by an arrow, and n *auxiliary ports* corresponding to the arity of the symbol.

We index ports clockwise from the principal port, and hence the orientation of an agent is not important. If $\mathsf{ar}(\alpha) = \mathsf{n}$, then an agent α is represented graphically in the following way:

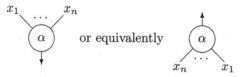

Note that this agent has been rotated (not reflected) and the ports are indexed in the same way. If $\mathsf{ar}(\alpha) = 0$, then the agent has no auxiliary ports, but it will always have a principal port.

In an interaction net, edges connect agents together at the ports such that there is at most one edge at each port (edges may connect two ports of the same agent). The ports of an agent that are not connected to another agent are called *free ports*. There are two special instances of a net that we should point out. A net may contain only edges (no agents); this is called a *wiring*, and the free extremities of the edges are also called ports. In this case, if there are n edges, then there are $2n$ free ports in the net. If a net contains neither edges nor agents, then it is the *empty net*. The *interface* of a net is its set of free ports.

Definition 7.2 (Interaction rule)

A pair of agents $(\alpha, \beta) \in \Sigma \times \Sigma$ connected together on their principal ports is called an *active pair*; this is the interaction net analogue of a redex, and it will be denoted $\alpha \bowtie \beta$.

An interaction rule $\alpha \bowtie \beta \Longrightarrow N$ in $\mathcal{R}$ is composed of an active pair on the left-hand side and a net N on the right-hand side. Rules must satisfy two strong conditions:

1. In an interaction rule, the left- and right-hand sides have the same interface; that is, all the free ports are preserved. The following diagram illustrates the idea, where N is any net built from Σ.

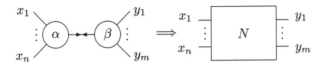

We remark that the net N may contain occurrences of the agents α and β. N can be just a wiring (but only if the number of free ports in the active pair is even), and if there are no free ports in the active pair, then the net N may be (but is not necessarily) the empty net.

2. In a set $\mathcal{R}$ of interaction rules, there is at most one rule for each unordered pair of agents (that is, only one rule for $\alpha \bowtie \beta$, which is the same as the rule for $\beta \bowtie \alpha$).

Interaction rules generate a reduction relation on nets, as shown below.

Definition 7.3

A reduction step using the rule $\alpha \bowtie \beta \Longrightarrow N$ replaces an occurrence of the active pair $\alpha \bowtie \beta$ by a net N. More precisely, we write $W \Longrightarrow W'$ if there is an active pair $\alpha \bowtie \beta$ in W and an interaction rule $\alpha \bowtie \beta \Longrightarrow N$ in $\mathcal{R}$ such that W' is the net obtained by replacing $\alpha \bowtie \beta$ in W with N (since N has the same interface as $\alpha \bowtie \beta$, there are no dangling edges after the replacement).

We write $\Longrightarrow$ for a single interaction step and $\Longrightarrow^*$ for the transitive reflexive closure of the relation $\Longrightarrow$. In other words, $N \Longrightarrow N'$ indicates that we can obtain N' from N by reducing one active pair, and $N \Longrightarrow^* N'$ indicates that there is a sequence of zero or more interaction steps that take us from N to N'.

We do not require a rule for each pair of agents, but if we create a net with an active pair for which there is no interaction rule, then this pair will not be reduced (it will be *blocked*).

It is important to note that the interface of the net is *ordered*. Adopting this convention, we can avoid labelling the free edges of a net. To give an example, we can write the rule

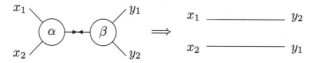

that connects x_1 with y_2 and x_2 with y_1 equivalently as the rule

$$x_1 \quad y_1 \qquad \qquad x_1 \text{———} y_2$$
$$\alpha \text{—} \beta \Longrightarrow$$
$$x_2 \quad y_2 \qquad \qquad x_2 \text{———} y_1$$

but in the latter the labelling is essential (the difference being that we have changed the order of the free ports of the net). We will always make an effort, at the cost of making the rules look more complicated, to ensure that the order of the edges is always preserved when we write a rule to avoid having to label the edges (adopting the same convention for nets as we did for agents).

An interaction net is in *full normal form* (we will often just call it normal form) if there are no active pairs. The notation $N \Downarrow N'$ indicates that there exists a finite sequence of interactions $N \Longrightarrow^* N'$ such that N' is a net in normal form. We say that a net N is *normalisable* if $N \Downarrow N'$; N is strongly normalisable if all sequences of interactions starting from N are finite.

As a direct consequence of the definition of interaction nets, in particular of the constraints on the rewrite rules, reduction is (strongly) commutative in the following sense: If two different reductions are possible in a net N (that is, $N \Longrightarrow N_1$ and $N \Longrightarrow N_2$), then there exists a net M such that N_1 and N_2 both reduce in one step to M: $N_1 \Longrightarrow M$ and $N_2 \Longrightarrow M$. This property is stronger than confluence (it is sometimes called strong confluence or the diamond property); it implies confluence. Consequently, we have the following result.

Proposition 7.4

Let N be a net in an interaction system $(\Sigma, \mathcal{R})$. Then:

1. If $N \Downarrow N'$, then all reduction sequences starting from N are terminating (N is strongly normalisable).

2. Normal forms are unique: If $N \Downarrow N'$ and $N \Downarrow N''$, then $N' = N''$.

Below we give an example of the implementation of two familiar operations using interaction nets.

Example 7.5

The following interaction rules define two ubiquitous agents, namely the *erasing* agent (ϵ), which deletes everything it interacts with, and the *duplicator* (δ), which copies everything.

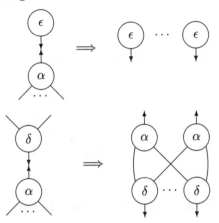

In the diagrams representing the rules, α denotes any agent. Indeed, there is one rule defining the interaction between ϵ and each agent α in Σ and also one rule for each pair $\delta \bowtie \alpha$.

According to the first rule above, the interaction between α and ϵ deletes the agent α and places erase agents on all the free edges of the agent. Note that if the arity of α is 0, then the right-hand side of the rule is the empty net; in this case the interaction marks the end of the erasing process. One particular case of this is when α is an ϵ agent itself. These rules provide the garbage collection mechanism for interaction nets.

In the second rule, we see that the α agent is copied, and the δ agents placed on the free edges can now continue copying the rest of the net.

7.2 Numbers and arithmetic operations

Natural numbers can be represented using 0 and a successor function, as described in previous chapters. For example, the number 3 is represented by $S(S(S(0)))$. Consider the following specification of the standard addition operation:

$$\begin{aligned} \mathsf{add}(0, y) &= y \\ \mathsf{add}(S(x), y) &= S(\mathsf{add}(x, y)) \end{aligned}$$

which indicates that adding 0 to any number y gives y as a result, and to add $x + 1$ to y, we need to compute $x + y$ and add 1.

To code this system into an interaction net program, we introduce three agents, corresponding to add, S, and 0. These are drawn as follows.

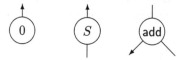

Next we must specify the rules of interaction. In this case, we can mirror the specification of addition given above. The two rules that we need are as follows:

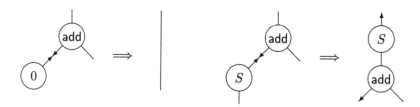

These rules trivially satisfy the requirements of preserving the interface for an interaction.

Consider the net corresponding to the term $\mathsf{add}(S(0), S(0))$:

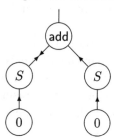

In this example, there is only one choice of reduction since at each step there is only one possible interaction that can take place. The complete sequence of reductions is shown below. The result is a net representing $S(S(0))$, as expected.

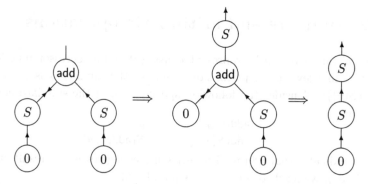

This example is rather too simple though to bring out the essential features of interaction nets. A more interesting example is the coding of the operation of multiplication, specified by

$$
\begin{aligned}
\mathsf{mult}(0, y) &= 0 \\
\mathsf{mult}(S(x), y) &= \mathsf{add}(\mathsf{mult}(x, y), y)
\end{aligned}
$$

To give an algorithm to multiply numbers using interaction nets, we need to introduce a new agent, m, to represent the multiplication operator. The interaction rules for this agent are more involved than those for add due to the fact that multiplication is not a linear operation (as was the case with addition). To keep in line with the definition of an interaction rule, we must preserve the interface. To illustrate this, here are the two rules for multiplication:

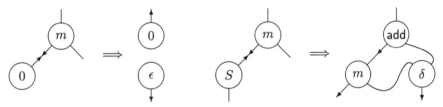

To preserve the interface, we have used the erasing and duplicating agents (ϵ and δ), that were introduced in Example 7.5.

This example illustrates one of the most interesting aspects of interaction nets. It is impossible to duplicate active pairs, and thus sharing of computation is naturally captured. Indeed, to duplicate a net, δ must be able to interact with all the agents in the net, but if α and β are connected on their principal ports, they cannot interact with δ and therefore cannot be copied.

Below we give another example of an operation on numbers and its definition using interaction nets.

Example 7.6

Consider the function that computes the maximum of two natural numbers:

$$
\begin{aligned}
\max(0, y) &= y \\
\max(x, 0) &= x \\
\max(S(x), S(y)) &= S(\max(x, y))
\end{aligned}
$$

The problem with this specification is that it is defined by cases on *both* of the arguments. If we follow the same ideas as in the previous examples, we would need two principal ports for the agent max, but this is not possible in interaction nets. However, we can transform the specification of max, introducing a new function max', to obtain an equivalent system where each operation is defined by cases on only one argument:

$$
\begin{aligned}
\max(0, y) &= y \\
\max(S(x), y) &= \max'(x, y) \\
\max'(x, 0) &= S(x) \\
\max'(x, S(y)) &= S(\max(x, y))
\end{aligned}
$$

The corresponding interaction rules are:

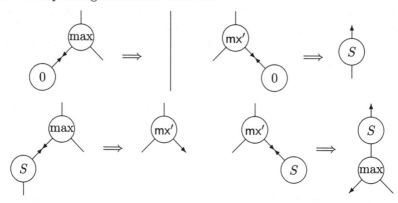

The definition of a system of interaction for computing the minimum of two numbers is left as an exercise (see Section 7.9).

This example suggests a method of compiling functions on numbers into interaction nets. Indeed, it is possible to compile all functional programs into interaction nets. Interaction nets are in fact a universal programming language, as we will see in the next section.

7.3 Turing completeness

To show that a model of computation is Turing complete, we have to prove that any computable function can be represented. In the case of interaction nets, this can be shown for instance by giving an encoding of combinatory logic (CL). Combinatory logic was introduced in Chapter 3 (see Exercise 11) as a system of combinators with constants, S and K, and two reduction rules with the same power as the λ-calculus. Let us recall the reduction rules:

$$
\begin{aligned}
K\, x\, y &\to x \\
S\, x\, y\, z &\to x\, z\, (y\, z)
\end{aligned}
$$

To represent CL as a system of interaction nets, we require an agent @ corresponding to application and several agents for the combinators. For example, the K combinator is encoded by introducing two agents, K_0 and K_1, and two interaction rules:

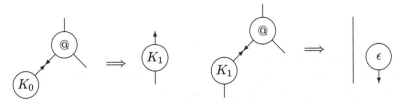

The combinator S can be defined in a similar way using three agents and three interaction rules; we leave it as an exercise.

Interaction nets have also been used to implement λ-calculus evaluators. Indeed, the first implementation of the optimal reduction strategy for the λ-calculus (that is, the strategy that makes the minimum number of β-reduction steps in order to normalise terms) used interaction nets. Interaction nets are also used in other (non-optimal, but in some cases more efficient) implementations of the λ-calculus.

Actually, if we restrict ourselves to linear λ-terms (see the definition of the linear λ-calculus in Exercise 10 of Chapter 3), we only need an application agent @ and an abstraction agent λ; variables can be encoded by wires. Then the β-reduction rule is simply encoded as follows:

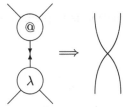

For general λ-terms, we have to introduce copying agents and erasing agents, as well as auxiliary agents to keep track of the scope of abstractions.

7.4 More examples: Lists

We can represent lists in interaction nets in different ways. For instance, we can build a list by using a binary agent cons to link the first element of the list to the rest of the list. The empty list can be represented with an agent nil. This representation of lists mimics the traditional specification of the list data structure in functional languages using constructors cons and nil. For instance, in a functional language, we could define list concatenation (the append function) as follows:

$$\begin{aligned} \mathsf{append}(\mathsf{nil}, l) &= l \\ \mathsf{append}(\mathsf{cons}(x, l), l') &= \mathsf{cons}(x, \mathsf{append}(l, l')) \end{aligned}$$

Using this representation of lists, the time required to concatenate two lists is proportional to the length of the lists (more precisely, with the definition above, it is proportional to the length of the first list).

A trivial encoding of lists and the concatenation operator in interaction nets, following the specification above, uses three agents: cons, nil, and append. However, if we use graphs instead of trees to represent lists, then we can obtain a more efficient implementation. The idea, to speed up the append function, is to have direct access to the first and last elements of the lists. Since interaction nets are general graphs, not just trees, this can be achieved simply by representing a list as a linked structure, using an agent Diff to hold pointers to the first and last elements of the list (the name comes from difference lists) and an agent cons as usual to link the internal elements.

The empty list, nil, is then encoded by the net:

The operation of concatenation is implemented in constant time with the net

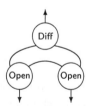

using an additional interaction rule that allows us to access the lists:

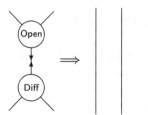

For example, we have the following reduction:

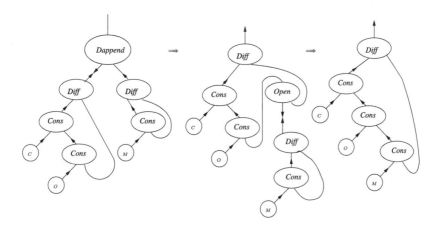

7.5 Combinators for interaction nets

The combinators S and K of combinatory logic provide a complete characterisation of computable functions; similarly, there is a universal set of combinators for interaction nets that uses three agents called δ, γ, and ϵ. In Figure 7.1, we give these three basic agents. The first two provide multiplexing operations (i.e., merging two wires into one), and the third is an erasing operation. All interaction nets can be built from these agents by simply wiring agents together.

Figure 7.1 Interaction combinators: γ, δ, and ϵ.

In Figure 7.2, we give the six interaction rules for this system. It is clear that the ϵ agent behaves as an erasing operation in that it consumes everything it interacts with. The multiplexing agents either annihilate each other (if they are the same agent), giving a wiring, or they mutually copy each other (if they are different). Note that the right-hand side in the final rule is the empty net.

This system of combinators is *universal* in the sense that any other interaction net system can be encoded using these combinators. There are other universal systems of combinators for interaction nets.

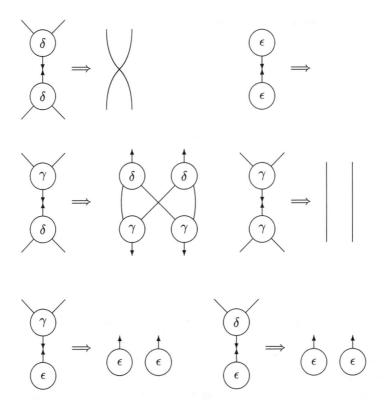

Figure 7.2 Interaction rules for the interaction combinators.

7.6 Textual languages and strategies for interaction nets

The graphical language of interaction nets is very natural, and diagrams are often easier to grasp than a textual description. However, a formal, textual account of interaction nets has many advantages: It simplifies the actual writing of programs (graphical editors are not always available), and static properties of nets, such as types, can be defined in a more concise way. Indeed, several textual notations for interaction nets have been devised. Below we describe three notations through an example before developing one of the notations into a full textual interaction calculus.

As a running example, consider the net given in Figure 7.3 and the interaction rule for β-reduction in the linear λ-calculus given in Section 7.3.

A natural textual notation for nets consists of listing all the agents, with their ports, using some convention. For instance, we could list the ports clock-

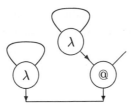

Figure 7.3 A λ-term represented as a net.

wise, starting from the principal port. Edges in the net can be represented by using the same port name. Using these conventions, the example net above is written

$$@(a, b, c), \lambda(a, d, d), \lambda(b, e, e)$$

since we have two λ agents and an application agent @. Note the repetition of name ports to define edges; for instance, in $\lambda(a, e, e)$, the repeated e indicates that there is a wire linking the two auxiliary ports of this λ agent.

The same notation can be used to represent interaction rules. For example, the interaction rule for linear β-reduction is written

$$@(a, b, c), \lambda(a, d, e) \Longrightarrow I(c, e), I(b, d)$$

where the symbol I is used to represent wirings (they are not attached to agents). Note that exactly the same ports are used on the left- and right-hand sides since interaction rules preserve the interface.

Another alternative is to use indices instead of names for ports, starting with the index 0 for the principal port. For the example net above, we use a set of agents:

$$\Sigma = \{@_1, \lambda_1, \lambda_2\}$$

The linear β-rule is written

$$(\lambda_i, @_j) \longrightarrow (\emptyset, \{\lambda_i.1 \equiv @_j.1, \lambda_i.2 \equiv @_j.2\})$$

and the example net is represented by

$$(\{@_1, \lambda_1, \lambda_2\}, \{@_1.0 \equiv \lambda_1.0, @_1.1 \equiv \lambda_2.0, \lambda_1.1 \equiv \lambda_1.2, \lambda_2.1 \equiv \lambda_2.2\})$$

A third alternative, which yields a more compact notation, is based on a representation of active pairs as equations. In this case, our example net is written

$$\lambda(a, a) = @(\lambda(b, b), c)$$

where the $=$ sign represents the connection between the principal port of the λ agent on the left-hand side and the principal port of the @ agent on the right-hand side (i.e., the equation encodes an active pair formed by a λ agent and an @ agent). The left-hand side $\lambda(a, a)$ of the equation indicates that both auxiliary ports of this λ agent are connected and similarly for $\lambda(b, b)$.

We follow the same approach to represent rules, but this time we use the symbol $\bowtie$ instead of $=$. For example, the linear β-reduction rule is written

$$@(x, y) \bowtie \lambda(x, y)$$

This notation, being more concise, is more suitable for the implementation of interaction net systems. The textual calculus of interaction that we present below is based on these ideas.

7.6.1 A textual interaction calculus

In this section, we describe a textual calculus for interaction nets that gives a formal account of the reduction process.

Interaction nets are strongly confluent, but as in all reduction systems, there exist different notions of strategies and normal forms (for instance, irreducible nets, or weak normal forms associated with lazy reduction strategies). We will see that these can be precisely defined in the calculus. Such strategies have applications for encodings of the λ-calculus, where interaction nets have had the greatest impact, and where a notion of a strategy is required to avoid non-termination.

We begin by describing the syntax of the interaction calculus.

Agents: Let Σ be a set of symbols $\alpha, \beta, \ldots$, each with a given *arity* (formally, we assume that there is a function $\mathsf{ar} \colon \Sigma \to \mathsf{Nat}$ that defines the arity of each symbol). An occurrence of a symbol will be called an *agent*. The arity of a symbol corresponds precisely to its number of auxiliary ports.

Names: Let N be a set of names x, y, z, etc. N and Σ are assumed disjoint.

Terms: A term is built using agents in Σ and names in N. Terms are generated by the grammar

$$t ::= x \mid \alpha(t_1, \ldots, t_n)$$

where $x \in N$, $\alpha \in \Sigma$, and $\mathsf{ar}(\alpha) = n$, with the restriction that each name can appear at most twice in a term. If $n = 0$, then we omit the parentheses.

If a name occurs twice in a term, we say that it is *bound*; otherwise it is *free*. Since free names occur exactly once, we say that terms are *linear*.

We write $\vec{t}$ for a list of terms $t_1, \ldots, t_n$.

A term of the form $\alpha(\vec{t})$ can be seen as a tree with edges between the leaves if names are repeated; the principal port of α is at the root, and the terms $t_1, \ldots, t_n$ are the subtrees connected to the auxiliary ports of α. Note that all the principal ports have the same orientation, and therefore there are no active pairs in such a tree.

Equations: If t and u are terms, then the (unordered) pair $t = u$ is an *equation*. Δ, $\Theta, \ldots$ will be used to range over multisets of equations. Examples of equations include $x = \alpha(\vec{t})$, $x = y$, $\alpha(\vec{t}) = \beta(\vec{u})$. Equations allow us to represent nets with active pairs.

Rules: Rules are pairs of terms written as $\alpha(\vec{t}) \bowtie \beta(\vec{u})$, where $(\alpha, \beta) \in \Sigma \times \Sigma$ is the active pair of the rule (that is, the left-hand side of the graphical interaction rule), and $\vec{t}, \vec{u}$ are terms. All names occur exactly twice in a rule, and there is at most one rule for each pair of agents.

Definition 7.7 (Names in terms)

The set $\mathcal{N}(t)$ of names of a term t is defined in the following way, which extends to multisets of equations and rules in the obvious way.

$$\begin{aligned} \mathcal{N}(x) &= \{x\} \\ \mathcal{N}(\alpha(t_1, \ldots, t_n)) &= \mathcal{N}(t_1) \cup \cdots \cup \mathcal{N}(t_n) \end{aligned}$$

Given a term, we can replace its free names by new names, provided the linearity restriction is preserved.

Definition 7.8 (Renaming)

The notation $t\{x \mapsto y\}$ denotes a renaming that replaces the free occurrence of x in t by a new name y. Note that since the name x occurs exactly once in the term, this operation can be implemented directly as an assignment, as is standard in the linear case. This notion extends to equations and multisets of equations in the obvious way.

More generally, we consider substitutions that replace free names in a term by other terms, always assuming that the linearity restriction is preserved.

Definition 7.9 (Substitution)

The notation $t\{x \mapsto u\}$ denotes a substitution that replaces the free occurrence of x by the term u in t. We only consider substitutions that preserve the linearity of the terms.

Note that renaming is a particular case of substitution. Substitutions have the following commutation property.

Proposition 7.10

Assume that $x \notin \mathcal{N}(v)$.

If $y \in \mathcal{N}(u)$, then $t\{x \mapsto u\}\{y \mapsto v\} = t\{x \mapsto u\{y \mapsto v\}\}$; otherwise $t\{x \mapsto u\}\{y \mapsto v\} = t\{y \mapsto v\}\{x \mapsto u\}$.

We now have all the machinery that we need to define nets in this calculus.

Definition 7.11 (Configurations)

A *configuration* is a pair $c = (\mathcal{R}, \langle \vec{t} \mid \Delta \rangle)$, where $\mathcal{R}$ is a set of rules, $\vec{t}$ a sequence $t_1, \ldots, t_n$ of terms, and Δ a multiset of equations. Each name occurs at most twice in c. If a name occurs once in c, then it is *free*; otherwise it is *bound*. For simplicity, we sometimes omit $\mathcal{R}$ when the set of rules used is clear from the context. We use c, c' to range over configurations. We call $\vec{t}$ the *head* or *observable interface* of the configuration.

Intuitively, $\langle \vec{t} \mid \Delta \rangle$ represents a net that we evaluate using $\mathcal{R}$, and Δ represents the active pairs and the renamings of the net. It is a multiset (i.e., a set where elements may be repeated since we may have several occurrences of the same active pair). The roots of the terms in the head of the configuration and the free names correspond to ports in the interface of the net. We work modulo α-equivalence for bound names as usual. Configurations that differ only in the names of the bound variables are equivalent since they represent the same net.

There is an obvious (although not unique) translation between the graphical representation of interaction nets and the configurations that we are using. Briefly, to translate a net into a configuration, we first orient the net as a collection of trees with all principal ports facing in the same direction. Each pair of trees connected at their principal ports is translated as an equation, and any tree whose root is free or any free port of the net goes in the head of the configuration. We give below a simple example to explain this translation.

Example 7.12

The usual encoding of the addition of natural numbers (see Section 7.2) uses the agents $\Sigma = \{0, S, \mathsf{add}\}$, where $\mathsf{ar}(0) = 0$, $\mathsf{ar}(S) = 1$, $\mathsf{ar}(\mathsf{add}) = 2$. The diagrams below illustrate the net representing the addition $1 + 0$ in the "usual" orientation and also with all the principal ports facing up.

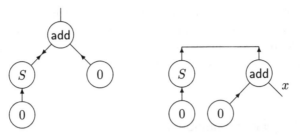

We then obtain the configuration $\langle x \mid S(0) = \mathsf{add}(x, 0)\rangle$, where the only port in the interface is x, which we put in the head of the configuration.

The reverse translation simply requires that we draw the trees for the terms, connect the common variables together, and connect the trees corresponding to the members of an equation together on their principal ports.

Definition 7.13 (Computation rules)

The operational behaviour of the system is given by the following set of computation rules:

Interaction: If $(\alpha(t'_1, \ldots, t'_n) \bowtie \beta(u'_1, \ldots, u'_m)) \in \mathcal{R}$, then

$$\langle \vec{t} \mid \alpha(t_1, \ldots, t_n) = \beta(u_1, \ldots, u_m), \Gamma\rangle \longrightarrow$$
$$\langle \vec{t} \mid t_1 = t'_1, \ldots, t_n = t'_n, u_1 = u'_1, \ldots, u_m = u'_m, \Gamma\rangle$$

Indirection: If $x \in \mathcal{N}(u)$, then

$$\langle \vec{t} \mid x = t, u = v, \Gamma\rangle \longrightarrow \langle \vec{t} \mid u\{x \mapsto t\} = v, \Gamma\rangle$$

Collect: If $x \in \mathcal{N}(\vec{t})$, then

$$\langle \vec{t} \mid x = u, \Delta\rangle \longrightarrow \langle \vec{t}\{x \mapsto u\} \mid \Delta\rangle$$

Multiset: If $\Theta \rightleftharpoons^* \Theta', \langle \vec{t_1} \mid \Theta'\rangle \longrightarrow \langle \vec{t_2} \mid \Delta'\rangle, \Delta' \rightleftharpoons^* \Delta$, then

$$\langle \vec{t_1} \mid \Theta\rangle \longrightarrow \langle \vec{t_2} \mid \Delta\rangle$$

These rules generate a reduction relation $\longrightarrow$ on configurations. We denote by $\longrightarrow^*$ the reflexive and transitive closure of $\longrightarrow$.

The first rule, Interaction, is the main computation rule. When using this rule, we always apply an α-renaming to get a copy of the interaction rule with all variables fresh. Indirection and Collect are administrative rules that we use to obtain a more compact textual representation and to make explicit the active pairs that may be created after applying the Interaction rule. The symbol $\rightleftharpoons$ above denotes an equivalence relation that states the irrelevance of the order of equations in the multiset as well as the order of the members in an equation.

The calculus makes evident the real cost of implementing an interaction step, which involves generating an instance (i.e., a new copy) of the right-hand side of the rule, plus renamings (rewirings). Of course this also has to be done when working in the graphical framework, even though it is often seen as an atomic step.

Example 7.14 (Natural numbers)

We show two different encodings of natural numbers and addition using the interaction calculus. The first encoding is the standard one, and the second is a more efficient version that offers a constant time addition operation.

1. Let $\Sigma = \{0, S, \mathsf{add}\}$ with $\mathsf{ar}(0) = 0$, $\mathsf{ar}(S) = 1$, $\mathsf{ar}(\mathsf{add}) = 2$, and $\mathcal{R}$:

$$\mathsf{add}(S(x), y) \quad \bowtie \quad S(\mathsf{add}(x, y))$$
$$\mathsf{add}(x, x) \qquad \bowtie \quad 0$$

As shown in Example 7.12, the net for 1+0 is given by the configuration $(\mathcal{R}, \langle a \mid \mathsf{add}(a, 0) = S(0)\rangle)$. One possible sequence of reductions for this net is the following:

$$\langle a \mid \mathsf{add}(a, 0) = S(0)\rangle$$
$$\longrightarrow \langle a \mid a = S(x'), y' = 0, 0 = \mathsf{add}(x', y')\rangle$$
$$\longrightarrow^* \langle S(x') \mid 0 = \mathsf{add}(x', 0)\rangle$$
$$\longrightarrow \langle S(x') \mid x'' = x', x'' = 0\rangle$$
$$\longrightarrow^* \langle S(0) \mid\rangle$$

2. Let $\Sigma = \{S, N, N^*\}$, $\mathsf{ar}(S) = 1$, $\mathsf{ar}(N) = \mathsf{ar}(N^*) = 2$. Numbers are represented as a list of S agents, where N is a constructor holding a link to the head and tail of the list. The number 0 is defined by the configuration $\langle N(x, x) \mid\rangle$, and in general n is represented by $\langle N(S^n(x), x) \mid\rangle$. The operation of addition can then be encoded by the configuration

$$\langle N(b, c), N^*(a, b), N^*(c, a)\rangle$$

which simply appends two numbers. We only need one interaction rule

$$N(a, b) \bowtie N^*(b, a)$$

which is clearly a constant time operation. To show how this works, we give an example of the addition of 1+1:

$$\langle N(b, c) \mid N(S(x), x) = N^*(a, b), N(S(y), y) = N^*(c, a)\rangle$$
$$\longrightarrow^* \langle N(b, c) \mid b = S(a), a = S(c)\rangle$$
$$\longrightarrow^* \langle N(S(S(c)), c) \mid\rangle$$

The interaction calculus is a Turing-complete model of computation, and therefore the halting problem (i.e., deciding whether a configuration produces an infinite reduction sequence) is undecidable in general. The following example shows that there are non-terminating configurations.

Example 7.15 (Non-termination)

Consider the net $\langle x, y \mid \alpha(x) = \beta(\alpha(y)) \rangle$ and the rule $\alpha(a) \bowtie \beta(\beta(\alpha(a)))$. The following non-terminating reduction sequence is possible:

$$
\begin{aligned}
\langle x, y \mid \alpha(x) = \beta(\alpha(y)) \rangle \quad &\longrightarrow \quad \langle x, y \mid x = a, \beta(\alpha(a)) = \alpha(y) \rangle \\
&\longrightarrow \quad \langle a, y \mid \beta(\alpha(a)) = \alpha(y) \rangle \\
&\longrightarrow \quad \cdots
\end{aligned}
$$

There is an obvious question to ask about this language with respect to the graphical formalism: Is it expressive enough to specify all interaction net systems? Under some assumptions, the answer is yes. There are in fact two restrictions. The first one is that there is no way of writing a rule with an active pair on the right-hand side. This is not a problem since it is possible to show that the class of interaction net systems where interaction rules are free of active pairs on the right-hand side has the same computation power as the class of rules that may include active pairs on the right-hand side. The second problem is the representation of interaction rules for active pairs without interface. In the calculus, an active pair without interface can only rewrite to the empty net. This is justified by the fact that disconnected nets can be ignored in this model of computation (only global computation rules can distinguish disconnected nets).

7.6.2 Properties of the calculus

This section is devoted to showing various properties of the reduction system defined by the rules Indirection, Interaction, Collect, and Multiset (see Definition 7.13). We have already mentioned these properties for the graphical formalism of interaction nets; they also hold for the calculus.

Proposition 7.16 (Confluence)

The relation $\longrightarrow$ is strongly confluent: If $c \longrightarrow d$ and $c \longrightarrow e$, for two different configurations d and e, then there is a configuration c' such that $d \longrightarrow c'$ and $e \longrightarrow c'$.

We write $c \Downarrow c'$ if and only if $c \longrightarrow^* c' \not\longrightarrow$. In other words, $c \Downarrow c'$ if c' is a normal form of c. As an immediate consequence of the previous property, we deduce that there is at most one normal form for each configuration: $c \Downarrow d$ and $c \Downarrow e$ implies $d = e$.

Although the calculus is non-terminating, as shown in Example 7.15, the restriction to the "administrative" rules Indirection and Collect is indeed terminating since applications of these rules reduce the number of equations in a configuration. Non-termination arises because of the Interaction rule (see Example 7.15), as expected.

7.6.3 Normal forms and strategies

Although we have stressed the fact that systems of interaction are strongly confluent, there are clearly many ways of obtaining the normal form (if one exists), and moreover there is scope for alternative kinds of normal forms, for instance those induced by weak reduction.

It is easy to characterise configurations that are fully reduced — we will call them full normal forms or simply normal forms. A configuration $(\mathcal{R}, \langle \vec{t} \mid \Delta \rangle)$ is in *full normal form* if Δ is empty or all the equations in Δ have the form $x = s$ with $x \in s$ or x free in $\langle \vec{t} \mid \Delta \rangle$.

We now define a weak notion of normal form, called the *interface normal form*, that is analogous to the notion of weak head normal form in the λ-calculus. This is useful in the implementation of the λ-calculus and functional programming languages to avoid non-terminating computations in disconnected nets.

Definition 7.17 (Interface normal form)

A configuration $(\mathcal{R}, \langle \vec{t} \mid \Delta \rangle)$ is in *interface normal form* (INF) if each t_i in $\vec{t}$ is of one of the following forms:

- $\alpha(\vec{s})$. For example, $\langle S(x) \mid x = Z \rangle$.

- x, where $x \in \mathcal{N}(t_j)$, $i \neq j$. This is called an *open path*. For example, $\langle x, x \mid \Delta \rangle$.

- x, where x occurs in a *cycle of principal ports* in Δ. For example, the configuration $\langle x \mid y = \alpha(\beta(y), x), \Delta \rangle$ has a cycle of principal ports (see the diagrams below).

Intuitively, an interaction net is in interface normal form when there are agents with principal ports on all of the observable interface, or, if there are ports in the interface that are not principal, then they will never become principal by reduction (since they are in an open path or a cycle).

The following diagrams illustrate the notion of an interface normal form. The first diagram, a subnet in the configuration $\langle \alpha(t_1, \ldots, t_n) \mid \Delta \rangle$, has an agent α with a free principal port in the interface; the terms t_i connected to the auxiliary ports of α represent the rest of the net, and there may be active pairs in this net if Δ is not empty. The second net contains an open path (through the agent δ).

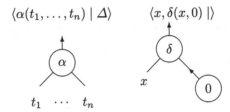

The following configurations are examples of nets with cycles of principal ports.

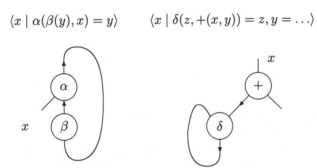

7.7 Extensions to model non-determinism

Interaction nets are a distributed model of computation in the sense that computations in a net can take place in parallel at any point in the net (no synchronisation is needed due to the strong confluence property of reductions in this model). However, interaction nets cannot model non-deterministic computations, which are a key ingredient of parallel programming languages.

To obtain an abstract model of computation capable of expressing non-deterministic choice, several extensions of interaction nets have been proposed. For instance, we could extend interaction net systems by

1. permitting the definition of several interaction rules for the same pair of

agents, in which case one of the rules will then be chosen at random when the two agents interact;

2. permitting edges that connect more than two ports; or

3. generalising the notion of an agent in order to permit interactions at several ports (in other words, multiple principal ports are permitted in an agent).

The first alternative is simple but not powerful enough to model a general notion of non-determinism. The second and third alternatives are more powerful. In fact, in the third case, it is sufficient to extend the interaction net paradigm of computing with just one agent with two principal ports. This distinguished agent represents ambiguous choice and is usually called amb. It is defined by the following interaction rules.

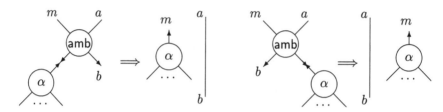

When an agent α has its principal port connected to a principal port of amb, an interaction can take place and the agent α arrives at the main output port of amb, which we called m in the diagram above. If in a net there are agents with principal ports connected to both principal ports of amb, the choice of the interaction rule to be applied is non-deterministic.

We illustrate the use of amb to program the *Parallel-or* function. This is an interesting Boolean operation that applies to two Boolean expressions and returns True if one of the arguments is True, independently of the computation taking place in the other argument. In other words, if both arguments have a Boolean value, this operation behaves exactly like an *or*, but even if one of the arguments does not return a value, as long as the other one is True, the Parallel-or function should return True. Since one of the arguments of Parallel-or may involve a partially defined Boolean function, the agent amb is crucial to detect the presence of a value True in one of the arguments. Below we specify this function using interaction nets extended with amb.

Example 7.18

The function *Parallel-or* must give a result True as soon as one of the arguments is True, even if the other one is undefined. Using an agent amb, we can easily encode *Parallel-or* with the net

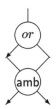

where the agent *or* represents the Boolean function *or*, defined (in standard interaction nets) by two interaction rules:

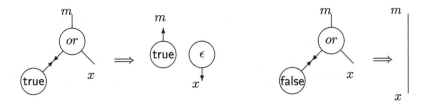

The model of computation based on interaction nets extended with amb is strictly more powerful than the interaction net model in the sense that it allows us to define non-deterministic computations or non-sequential functions, such as Parallel-or.

In order to define parallel processes explicitly and facilitate the analysis of the behaviour of concurrent systems, in the next chapter we will present a formalism based on a notion of communication between processes.

7.8 Further reading

Yves Lafont's article [28] provides an introduction to interaction nets and many examples of their use. For more information on interaction combinators, and a proof of universality, we refer the reader to [29]. We refer to [42] for implementations of interaction nets. The compact textual notation for interaction nets described in this chapter was suggested by Lafont in his introductory article [28]; the calculus based on this notation is developed in [16]. We also refer the reader to [16] for more notions of normal forms and strategies of evaluation.

7.9 Exercises

1. Using interaction nets, define the following functions on numbers represented with 0 and S (successor):

   – is-zero, which produces a result True if the number is 0 and False otherwise;

   – min, which computes the minimum of two numbers;

   – factorial, which computes the factorial of a number.

2. Specify an interaction system that generates infinite computations (loops).

3. Complete the definition of the interaction system for combinatory logic given in Section 7.3. More precisely, define the agents and rules needed to define the S combinator (it can be defined with three agents and three rules).

4. a) Give an interaction system to compute the Boolean function *and*.

   b) Draw the interaction net representing the expression

   $$(True \ and \ False) \ and \ True$$

   How many reductions are needed to fully normalise this net?

   c) Modify the system so that the result is *True* if and only if both arguments have the same value (i.e., both *True* or both *False*).

5. Give a representation of lists in interaction nets, and use it to implement a function that interleaves the elements of two given lists. More precisely, define an interaction system that, given two lists l_1 and l_2, produces a new list containing the elements of l_1 interleaved with those of l_2. For instance, the result of interleaving [0, 2, 4] and [1, 3] is the list [0, 1, 2, 3, 4].

6. Textual rules defining addition were given in Example 7.14. Can you write the textual version of the rules for multiplication given in Section 7.2?

7. Explain why interaction nets are not suitable as a model for non-deterministic computations.

8. Define the function Parallel-and using the agent amb. Parallel-and is a binary Boolean operator returning the value False whenever one of the arguments is False and True when both are True.

8
Concurrency

In the previous chapters, we described several models of computation that reflect different ways in which the process of computation can be understood. All these different abstract models of computation share one characteristic: The goal is to express sequential algorithms. To describe the meaning of a sequential program, we can use an operational approach in which we see an algorithm as a black box transforming some given input data into the desired output. However, in some contexts, for example when describing the behaviour of an operating system, this input-output abstraction is not well suited. The final result of the algorithm might not be of interest, or the notion of "final" might not even apply. Indeed, an operating system does stop running in some cases, typically when we shut down our computer, but then we are not expecting a "result" from the computation.

Concurrent systems of computation differ from sequential ones in three main aspects:

– Non-termination:

Although sequential programs that do not terminate are usually uninteresting, in the concurrent case most interesting systems are actually non-terminating. In this context, we need a more general notion of algorithm that associates a computational meaning also to programs that do not stop.

– Non-determinism:

Sequential algorithms are usually deterministic, and each execution of the same program with the same data in the same abstract machine produces the same results. However, in some cases non-determinism is useful (most programming languages, even sequential ones, allow programmers to simulate non-determinism by using, for instance, a random number generator).

– Interference:

In a concurrent system, the meaning of a program may depend on the behaviour of the other programs that are being executed concurrently, unlike in sequential systems, where the meaning of a program is determined by the program itself and the abstract machine for which it was written. For instance, if several programs are running in parallel and they are all trying to read and write the same record in a database, then, in order to guarantee the consistency of the database, access to records must be controlled, as the following example of interference shows.

Example 8.1

Suppose that a university stores the contact details of students in a file containing a record for each student. Suppose the fields in each record include the name and the address of the student, and we have a record containing

```
Name: "Claire", Address: "Belgravia"
```

Consider two processes, P1 and P2, running concurrently and executing the following operations on Claire's record, with the aim of adding more details to the address (we use the symbol + to denote string concatenation).

Process P1:

```
Address := "Belgravia, London";
```

```
Print record
```

Process P2:

```
Address := Address + ", London";
```

```
Print record
```

Seen as sequential programs, P1 and P2 can be considered equivalent: they both replace the contents of the address field in this record by the string

$$\text{“Belgravia, London”}$$

and print it.

However, in a concurrent system, if these processes are running in parallel, the final result depends on the order in which the instructions are executed. We may have some unexpected results if, for instance, P1's first instruction is followed by P2's first instruction. In this case, the execution of a printing instruction for this record will show

Claire, Belgravia, London, London

which is not the intended result.

Concurrent programs should be carefully written to avoid interference.

Concurrent systems share a number of general characteristics, including the following notions:

- *Process:* Any entity that describes computation, or that is capable of performing computations, is usually called a process; the words agent, component, or thread are sometimes used instead of the word process.

- *Communication:* Processes that are running in parallel can exchange data, or information in general, by sending and receiving messages. In some cases, the communication links are fixed, whereas in other cases there is some degree of flexibility and the system can create new communication channels or change the ones available.

- *Interaction:* As a result of the fact that processes are running concurrently, their collective behaviour may depend on each other's individual actions. Processes can interact, either in a positive way to achieve a common goal or in an unintended way as in the case of the interference described in Example 8.1.

There is another important aspect of concurrent systems: their observable behaviour. This replaces the notion of "result" associated with a sequential algorithm. Since in many cases there is no result associated with a concurrent program, the important feature of such a system is its behaviour whilst running. In other words, we should be able to observe changes during the execution of the concurrent program, and we can compare concurrent systems by observing their behaviour and comparing the observations.

Some examples may help to illustrate these ideas. We can identify the notions described above in the concurrent systems that we encounter in everyday situations. For example, the following are concurrent systems in the sense described above:

- A vending machine for drinks and a person using the machine can be seen as a concurrent system. Although in this chapter we will be focusing on computer systems rather than physical systems, it is still interesting to see that the same notions apply. We can see the vending machine and the user as two processes that communicate (albeit in a simple, not very flexible way) and interact in order to attain a common goal. The behaviour of the system is easy to observe: Lights indicate whether different drinks are available, buttons can be used to select drinks, the machine accepts coins, the machine delivers a drink, etc. And, of course, if two vending machines for drinks are available, our choice is likely to be based on our observations.

— The World Wide Web is a good example of a concurrent system where the notion of communication is very flexible. New communication links can be created, and existing links can be removed.

— Another example of a concurrent system where the communication channels are not fixed is an airport. More precisely, an airport's control tower and the collection of aircraft that at any time are under the control of the tower can be seen as a concurrent system. In this case, an aircraft might establish a communication link with the tower in order to land at the airport, and after the landing has taken place, the channel may be destroyed. Interaction between different aircraft is possible, although not always expected, and interaction between the tower and the aircraft is of course expected.

8.1 Specifying concurrent systems

In the previous section, we identified the main features that distinguish a concurrent system from a sequential one. In order to specify a concurrent system, we need a formalism that allows us to define these different features. In particular, since in the case of a concurrent system we are interested in the behaviour of the system as opposed to its final outputs, we need a formalism that allows us to specify behavioural aspects of the system.

Transition diagrams are one of the tools used for the description of processes in concurrent systems. We can see these diagrams as a particular kind of automaton, where the transitions describe the possible actions of the machine. There is also a textual view of these diagrams: In Chapter 2, we associated a formal language with a finite automaton; similarly, it is possible to associate an algebra of expressions with a transition diagram.

Specifically, in this chapter we will use *labelled transition systems* to specify concurrent systems. These are graphs where nodes represent the state of the system and edges correspond to transitions between states, labelled by actions. Before giving the formal definition, we present some examples to illustrate the idea.

Example 8.2

Consider a simple version of a vending machine that can deliver coffee or tea. Assume that, after introducing a coin, the machine allows us to select the drink by pushing the tea or the coffee button. The machine will then produce the required drink and deliver it, after which it is again ready to sell another drink.

The behaviour of this machine can be specified using a labelled transition diagram, as depicted in Figure 8.1.

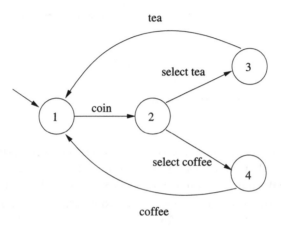

Figure 8.1 Labelled transition diagram for a vending machine.

The diagram in Figure 8.1 is similar to the diagrams used in Chapter 2 to recognise regular languages, and we have used the same notation to indicate the initial state (a small arrow). However, in the case of finite automata, the goal is to describe a formal language, whereas now we are describing the actions the machine can do at each state. In this sense, the properties of labelled transition diagrams are different from the properties of finite automata. For instance, the diagram in Figure 8.2, seen as a non-deterministic finite automaton, defines the same language as the automaton in Figure 8.1, but in fact, as a description of a vending machine, it specifies a behaviour that is very different from the previous one. When in the initial state the user inserts a coin, the machine will move in a non-deterministic way either to a state in which it can produce a coffee or to a state in which it can produce a tea. In other words, whereas in the machine specified in Figure 8.1 it is the user who chooses the drink, in the second machine the choice is done internally. After we insert a coin, all we know is that a drink will be delivered, but it could be either a coffee or a tea and there is no way to know in advance which one the machine will produce!

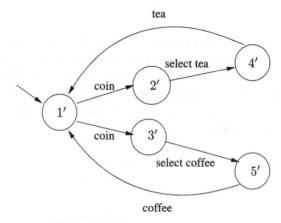

Figure 8.2 Labelled transition diagram for a non-deterministic vending machine.

The question then naturally arises as to when two such systems are equivalent. The fact that processes of interest may be non-terminating or non-deterministic rules out a notion of equivalence based on the results obtained, as is standard for sequential programs, where two functions f and g are equivalent if they produce the same output for each given input, formally

$$f = g \iff \forall x. f(x) = g(x).$$

Also, as the previous example shows, it is not useful to compare the automata by comparing their associated languages. Moreover, it is easy to see that the fact that two systems are defined by diagrams with a similar shape does not guarantee that they have the same behaviour. What then would be a reasonable notion of equivalence?

Indeed, we should not forget that the specification of a concurrent system is mainly a description of its *behaviour*. It is then natural to say that two systems are equivalent if they have the same behaviour. We mentioned in the previous section that one of the main characteristics of this notion of behaviour is that it is *observable*: We are interested in the observable behaviour of the system. To give a concrete example, we could say that two vending machines that offer the same drinks at the same price (i.e., two machines for which all the relevant observations coincide) are equivalent, even if internally they are built in different ways.

Below we will define this notion of behavioural equivalence formally using a bisimilarity relation, but in order to do that, we need a formal definition of labelled transition systems.

Let *Act* be an alphabet; i.e., a denumerable (finite or infinite) set of symbols, called *labels*. The alphabets we will use in our examples are composed of two kinds of labels, called *actions* and *co-actions*:

$$Act = \mathcal{N} \cup \overline{\mathcal{N}}$$

For example, in the case of the vending machine, the set of actions is

$$\mathcal{N} = \{\text{coin}, \text{coffee}, \text{tea}, \ldots\}$$

and the co-actions are

$$\overline{\mathcal{N}} = \{\overline{\text{coin}}, \overline{\text{coffee}}, \overline{\text{tea}}, \ldots\}$$

Actions and co-actions represent two complementary views of an interaction between two processes. This will be useful in systems composed of several processes that need to work in a synchronised way.

We are now ready to define labelled transition systems.

Definition 8.3 (Labelled transition system)

A labelled transition system, with labels in *Act*, is a pair (Q, T), where

− Q is a set of *states* and

− T is a *transition relation*; that is, a ternary relation between a state, a label, and another state: $T \subseteq (Q \times Act \times Q)$.

We write $q \longrightarrow^a q'$ if $(q, a, q') \in T$ and say that in the state q the process can perform the action a and move to state q'.

Each process in a concurrent system will be specified as a labelled transition system. It is not necessary to define an initial state, and in general there are no final states in labelled transition systems. Indeed, in many cases there is no distinguished starting state, every state can be considered as an initial one, and every state can be a final state.

We can now go back to the problem of defining process equivalence.

8.2 Simulation and bisimulation

Given two labelled transition systems, we start by defining a relation between their states. In fact, it does not matter whether the states belong to the same automaton or to different ones (in any case, an automaton can be composed of several disconnected parts).

Intuitively, we would like to say that two states are equivalent if their observations coincide. More precisely, two states are equivalent if whenever an action is possible in one of them it is also possible in the other, and after this action takes place the resulting states are also equivalent. Formally, we define the notion of *strong simulation* as follows.

Definition 8.4 (Strong simulation)

Let (Q, T) be a labelled transition system on *Act*. A binary relation S on Q is a *strong simulation* if pSq implies that, for each a in *Act* such that $p \longrightarrow^a p'$, there exists q' in Q such that $q \longrightarrow^a q'$ and $p'Sq'$.

If pSq holds, we say that q *simulates* p.

The idea is that if pSq holds, any transition that can be done from the state p can also be done from q, and the resulting states are still in the relation.

Example 8.5

Consider the diagrams in Figures 8.1 and 8.2. The relation

$$S = \{(1', 1), (2', 2), (3', 2), (4', 3), (5', 4)\}$$

is a strong simulation. We can check that, for each pair $(p, q) \in S$ and for each action a such that $p \longrightarrow^a p'$, there is a transition $q \longrightarrow^a q'$ such that $(p', q') \in S$. For instance, take $(3', 2)$. There is only one possible action at state $3'$ in Figure 8.2, namely select coffee, with a transition $3' \longrightarrow^{\text{select coffee}} 5'$. Similarly, in Figure 8.1, there is a transition $2 \longrightarrow^{\text{select coffee}} 4$ and the pair $(5', 4)$ is in S as required.

The fact that we can build a strong simulation as above indicates that the deterministic vending machine can simulate the non-deterministic one. The reverse is not true: The non-deterministic machine cannot simulate the original one. For this, it is sufficient to prove that there is no strong simulation containing the pair $(2, i')$ for any state i' in the non-deterministic machine. In other words, the behaviour of the original machine in state 2 is observably different from the behaviour of the non-deterministic machine, whichever state we consider.

The strong simulation relation defined above allows us to compare processes, but it does not define an equivalence relation. To obtain an equivalence relation, we need simulations in both directions; this is the essence of the notion of strong bisimulation.

Definition 8.6 (Strong bisimulation)

Let (Q, T) be a labelled transition system on Act and S a binary relation on Q. We say that S is a *strong bisimulation* if S and S^{-1} are strong simulations, where S^{-1} denotes the inverse of S (i.e., $pS^{-1}q$ if qSp).

We will write $p \sim q$ if there is a strong bisimulation S such that $(p, q) \in S$, and in this case we will say that p and q are *bisimilar*. The relation $\sim$ is called *strong bisimilarity*.

According to the definition above, $\sim$ is the union of all the strong bisimulations — it contains all the pairs (p, q) such that pSq for some strong bisimulation S.

The strong bisimilarity relation defined above is also a strong bisimulation, and it is an equivalence relation (indeed, it is the equivalence relation we were looking for).

Proposition 8.7

1. The relation $\sim$ is reflexive, symmetric, and transitive:

   For all p, $p \sim p$.

   For all p, q, if $p \sim q$, then $q \sim p$.

   For all p, q, r, if $p \sim q$ and $q \sim r$, then $p \sim r$.

2. The relation $\sim$ is a strong bisimulation.

In the rest of the chapter, we define a simple programming language that can be used to define individual processes (Section 8.3) and then show how this language can be extended to model process communication and interaction (Section 8.4). We briefly describe an alternative view of concurrency, based on the chemical metaphor, in Section 8.5.

8.3 A language to write processes

We can associate a process expression with a labelled transition diagram. A language of expressions will be useful to program concurrent systems where each component can be seen as a process (i.e., an expression) and several processes can be combined via suitable operators.

Consider a set of identifiers that will be used as names for processes

$$Id = \{A, B, C, \ldots\}$$

and a set of labels

$$Act = \mathcal{N} \cup \overline{\mathcal{N}} = \{a, b, c, \ldots\} \cup \{\overline{a}, \overline{b}, \overline{c}, \ldots\}$$

We will also assume that there is a denumerable set of variables $x_1, \ldots, x_n, \ldots$.

Definition 8.8 (Process expression)

Process expressions are generated by the grammar

$$P ::= A\langle \alpha_1, \ldots, \alpha_n \rangle \mid \Sigma_{i \in I} \, \alpha_i.P_i$$

where the symbols α_i range over variables or labels, A is a process identifier, I is a finite set of indices, and in $\alpha_i.P_i$ we say that α_i is a *prefix*.

The two kinds of process expressions generated by the grammar above are called *named processes* and *sums*, respectively. A named process consists of a process identifier and a list of parameters, written $A\langle \alpha_1, \ldots, \alpha_n \rangle$, and a sum is a finite set of expressions of the form $\alpha_i.P_i$, where each P_i is a process expression. In the latter case, if $I = \emptyset$, then $\Sigma_{i \in I}\alpha_i.P_i$ is written 0, representing the inert process that does not perform any computation.

To each process identifier A we will associate an expression, using an equation that we call the *definition* of A,

$$A(x_1, \ldots, x_n) = P_A$$

where P_A is a sum that can use the variables $x_1, \ldots, x_n$.

The intuition behind a definition such as the one above is that each time the process A is used in a program (that is, each time an expression of the form $A\langle a_1, \ldots, a_n \rangle$ occurs), it can be replaced by the expression P_A, where each occurrence of x_i is replaced by a_i. The latter will be written $P_A\{x_1 \mapsto a_1, \ldots, x_n \mapsto a_n\}$, where the expression $\{x_1 \mapsto a_1, \ldots, x_n \mapsto a_n\}$ is a *substitution*.

For this reason, in the context of an equation $A(x_1, \ldots, x_n) = P_A$, the expression $A\langle a_1, \ldots, a_n \rangle$ is equivalent to $P_A\{x_1 \mapsto a_1, \ldots, x_n \mapsto a_n\}$, and, more generally, two expressions P and Q are considered equivalent, written $P \equiv Q$, if the equality $P = Q$ can be derived in the equational theory generated by the equations.

For example, in the context of the equation

$$A(x) = x.A\langle x \rangle$$

we can derive the following equivalences:

$$A\langle a \rangle \equiv a.A\langle a \rangle \equiv a.a.A\langle a \rangle$$

We now have all the ingredients to define processes.

Definition 8.9 (Process)

A process is defined by a process expression (see Definition 8.8) together with the equations that define the process identifiers occurring in the expression.

To each process we can associate a labelled transition system (Q, T) on *Act* as follows:

– The set Q of states corresponds to the set of (sub)expressions in the process.

– There is a transition $\Sigma_{i \in I} \, \alpha_i.P_i \longrightarrow^{\alpha_j} P_j$ for each $j \in I$.

The example below illustrates the idea.

Example 8.10 (Buffer)

Consider a buffer of size two that we see as a container where we can store two items. The actions associated with the buffer are only of two kinds. We can either put an item in the buffer if there is space for it or take an item out if the buffer is not empty. In the latter case, if the buffer is full, we assume that any one of the items stored will be removed.

In this case, we can model the buffer using an alphabet that contains the actions

$$\mathcal{N} = \{in, out\}$$

We now have to define the associated process. For this, we will first use a labelled transition system to specify the behaviour of the buffer. The set of states should include the empty buffer, the buffer that contains one value, and a full buffer. Let us call the states B_0 (empty buffer), B_1 (buffer containing one item), and B_2 (full buffer).

We have the following transitions at each state:

$B_0 \longrightarrow^{in} B_1$

$B_1 \longrightarrow^{in} B_2, \; B_1 \longrightarrow^{out} B_0$

$B_2 \longrightarrow^{out} B_1$

We can then associate the following definitions with the identifiers B_0, B_1, and B_2:

$$B_0(in) = in.B_1\langle in, out \rangle$$
$$B_1(in, out) = out.B_0\langle in \rangle + in.B_2\langle out \rangle$$
$$B_2(out) = out.B_1\langle in, out \rangle$$

The system is initialised by defining the process $Buffer = B_0\langle in \rangle$.

8.4 A language for communicating processes

Using the language of expressions defined in the previous section, we can specify the behaviour of an individual process. In order to specify a system of concurrent processes, we need to extend the language, so that communication and interaction between processes can be defined. With this aim, we introduce two new syntactic constructions:

– Parallel composition, written $P_1|P_2$, allows us to specify two processes, P_1 and P_2, and combine them by executing them in parallel. The binary operator of parallel composition, denoted by $|$, is associative and commutative, so we can compose several processes simply by writing $P_1|P_2|P_3|\ldots$.

– The restriction operator allows us to encapsulate a name to avoid name clashes when several individual processes that could use the same alphabet are combined together. We write $\nu a.P$ to indicate that the name a is private in P and will be distinguished from any other a used in the processes composed with P. This is easy to achieve by considering ν as a binder and defining process expressions as equivalence classes modulo renamings of bound names (for instance, in the same way as λ is a binder and λ-terms are defined modulo α-equivalence). We will sometimes abbreviate $\nu a.\nu b.P$ as $\nu ab.P$.

Two processes that are running in parallel can interact by performing an action and the associated co-action. For instance, in the example of the vending machine, if we consider the machine as a process and a user as another one, interaction can take place by an action performed by the user (e.g., introducing a coin) with the associated co-action (accepting the coin) performed by the machine. As mentioned previously, actions and co-actions are just two different views of the interaction, so it makes sense to synchronise parallel processes in this way. More precisely, if P and Q are processes running in parallel, where P performs a transition labelled by a and Q performs a transition labelled by $\bar{a}$, we will say that P and Q have interacted and as a result the system as a whole has changed state.

This interaction can be specified operationally

$$\text{If } P \longrightarrow^a P' \text{ and } Q \longrightarrow^{\overline{a}} Q' \text{ then } P|Q \longrightarrow^\tau P'|Q'$$

which states that the system formed by the concurrent processes P and Q has changed state after the processes have performed complementary actions. Notice that the transition out of $P|Q$ has a special label, τ. Transitions labelled by τ are called τ-transitions or *silent transitions* because if we consider the system as a black box, we cannot observe the individual actions taking place in P or Q. In other words, in a τ-transition there is no interaction with the environment, the interaction is internal.

To take into account τ-transitions, we extend the set *Act* used in the definition of individual processes by adding a distinguished label τ.

Summarising, the set of expressions in the extended language includes the process expressions defined previously (in Definition 8.8) and all the expressions that can be obtained by parallel composition and restriction as indicated below.

Definition 8.11 (Extended process language)

The syntax of the expressions in the concurrent process language is defined by the grammar

$$P ::= A\langle \alpha_1, \ldots, \alpha_n \rangle \ | \ \Sigma_{i \in I} \alpha_i . P_i \ | \ P_1 | P_2 \ | \ \nu a . P$$

where the α_is range over variables or labels from the alphabet *Act*:

$$Act = \mathcal{N} \cup \overline{\mathcal{N}} \cup \{\tau\} \ \text{ and } \ \mathcal{N} = \{a, b, c, \ldots\}$$

We work modulo a congruence $\equiv$ on expressions (i.e., an equivalence relation closed by context) generated by

– renaming (i.e., α-conversion) of restricted names;

– commutativity and associativity of the sum;

– commutativity and associativity of parallel composition;

– neutral element: $P|0 \equiv P$;

– $\nu a.(P|Q) \equiv P|\nu a.Q$ if a is not free in P;

– $\nu a.0 \equiv 0$, $\nu ab.P \equiv \nu ba.P$;

– $A\langle b_1, \ldots, b_n \rangle \equiv P_A\{a_1 \mapsto b_1, \ldots, a_n \mapsto b_n\}$ if $A(a_1, \ldots, a_n) = P_A$.

The transition relation extends in the natural way to expressions that use parallel composition and restriction operators. We define below the extended relation, which we still call T since there is no ambiguity. In the definition of transitions, we use α to denote any label in $Act = \mathcal{N} \cup \overline{\mathcal{N}} \cup \{\tau\}$.

Definition 8.12 (Extended transition relation)

The transition relation is generated by the following rules:

$$
\begin{array}{lll}
(Sum) & M + \alpha.P & \longrightarrow^{\alpha} \; P \\
(Def) & A\langle a_1, \ldots, a_n \rangle & \longrightarrow^{\alpha} \; P' \quad \text{if } A(x_1, \ldots, x_n) = P_A \text{ and} \\
& & \qquad P_A\{x_1 \mapsto a_1, \ldots, x_n \mapsto a_n\} \longrightarrow^{\alpha} P' \\
(Reaction) & P|Q & \longrightarrow^{\tau} \; P'|Q' \quad \text{if } P \longrightarrow^{\alpha} P' \text{ and } Q \longrightarrow^{\overline{\alpha}} Q' \\
& & \qquad \text{where } \alpha \neq \tau \\
(Par) & P|Q & \longrightarrow^{\alpha} \; P'|Q \quad \text{if } P \longrightarrow^{\alpha} P' \\
(Restr) & \nu a.P & \longrightarrow^{\alpha} \; \nu a.P' \quad \text{if } P \longrightarrow^{\alpha} P' \text{ and } \alpha \neq a, \alpha \neq \overline{a}
\end{array}
$$

Note that, since we are working on equivalence classes, if for a given expression P there is a transition $P \longrightarrow^{\alpha} P'$ according to the definition above, then also $Q \longrightarrow^{\alpha} Q'$ for any Q and Q' such that $P \equiv Q$ and $P' \equiv Q'$. In particular, if $Q \longrightarrow^{a} Q'$, then $P|Q \longrightarrow^{a} P|Q'$ using the rule (Par).

We give an example below.

Example 8.13

Let P be the expression

$$
\nu b.((a.b.P_1 + b.P_2 + c.0) \mid \overline{a}.0) \mid (\overline{b}.P_3 + \overline{a}.P_4)
$$

Using (Sum), $(a.b.P_1 + b.P_2 + c.0) \longrightarrow^{a} b.P_1$, and also $\overline{a}.0 \longrightarrow^{\overline{a}} 0$. Therefore, using $(Reaction)$, we deduce

$$
((a.b.P_1 + b.P_2 + c.0) \mid \overline{a}.0) \longrightarrow^{\tau} b.P_1 \mid 0
$$

Hence $P \longrightarrow^{\tau} \nu b.(b.P_1|0) \mid (\overline{b}.P_3 + \overline{a}.P_4)$ using $(Restr)$ and (Par), and the latter expression is congruent with $\nu b.(b.P_1) \mid (\overline{b}.P_3 + \overline{a}.P_4)$, so

$$
P \longrightarrow^{\tau} \nu b.(b.P_1) \mid (\overline{b}.P_3 + \overline{a}.P_4)
$$

Now, although b and $\overline{b}$ are prefixes of parallel processes in this expression, the reaction cannot take place because b is a private name in one of the components; we could have written equivalently

$$
P \longrightarrow^{\tau} \nu c.(c.P_1) \mid (\overline{b}.P_3 + \overline{a}.P_4)
$$

Note that the transition relation is not confluent: For a given expression, there may be several different irreducible forms. For instance, in the example above, the initial expression P can be written as

$$
\nu d.((a.d.P_1 + d.P_2 + c.0) \mid \overline{a}.0) \mid (\overline{b}.P_3 + \overline{a}.P_4)
$$

which is congruent with

$$\nu d.((a.d.P_1 + d.P_2 + c.0) \mid (\overline{b}.P_3 + \overline{a}.P_4) \mid \overline{a}.0)$$

and we have a transition $P \longrightarrow^\tau \nu d.(d.P_1 \mid P_4 \mid \overline{a}.0)$.

Indeed, when several τ-transitions are possible, there is no pre-established order for them; this non-deterministic aspect of the transition relation is one of the features of concurrent systems.

Since the extended transition relation includes τ-transitions, which cannot be observed, the definition of bisimulation is extended to ignore silent transitions.

Let $P \Rightarrow^\alpha Q$, where $\alpha \neq \tau$, denote a sequence of transitions from P to Q containing any number of τ steps and at least one α-transition. More precisely, we write $P \Rightarrow^\alpha Q$ if there is a sequence of transitions $P \longrightarrow^{\tau*} P' \longrightarrow^\alpha Q' \longrightarrow^{\tau*} Q$. Bisimulation is defined as in Definition 8.6 but using $\Rightarrow$ instead of $\longrightarrow$; in this way, bisimilarity equates processes that have the same behaviour when we do not consider τ transitions.

The language of concurrent process expressions satisfies the following properties.

Proposition 8.14

– For each expression P, there are only a finite number of transitions $P \longrightarrow^\alpha P'$ available (i.e., the transition diagram is finitely branching).

– The structural congruence $\equiv$ is a strong bisimulation and thus is included in the bisimilarity relation; that is, $P \equiv Q$ implies $P \sim Q$.

We finish this section with the specification of a bidirectional channel using the language of concurrent process expressions defined above.

Example 8.15 (Bidirectional channel)

A channel can be seen as a buffer where the sender deposits a message on one end and the receiver retrieves the message from the other end. In a bidirectional channel, both ends can be senders or receivers.

We start by defining a bidirectional channel of size 1. In this case, the maximum number of messages in the channel at any time is 1. Let us call the channel C and assume the points connected by the channel are called A and B, as depicted in Figure 8.3.

In the process calculus, we will represent the channel C as a process and will denote by a the action of sending a message from A and by $\overline{a'}$ the action

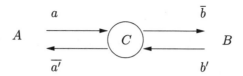

Figure 8.3 Bidirectional channel.

of receiving a message at A (similarly, b and $\overline{b'}$ denote sending and receiving at B). The process C can be defined by the equation

$$C(a, a', b, b') = a.\overline{b}.C + b'.\overline{a'}.C$$

The transition diagram is given in Figure 8.4. It is easy to see in the diagram that the following sequence of transitions is permitted, allowing messages to pass from left to right through the channel:

$$C \longrightarrow^a \overline{b}.C \longrightarrow^{\overline{b}} C$$

Similarly, messages can be sent from right to left.

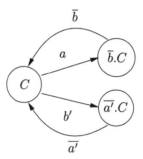

Figure 8.4 Transition diagram for a bidirectional channel.

We can compose several channels; for instance, let D be another bidirectional channel of size 1, connecting B with E. Assume D is defined by the equation

$$D(b, b', e, e') = C\langle b, b', e, e' \rangle$$

We can now define the channel CD connecting A with E by composing C and D using the expression

$$CD(a, a', e, e') = \nu bb'.(C\langle a, a', b, b' \rangle | D\langle b, b', e, e' \rangle)$$

The channels C and D are now "joined" at B. The fact that B is no longer an "open end" is represented by the restriction, which makes the names b and b' private to C and D.

8.5 Another view of concurrency: The chemical metaphor

Around fifteen years ago, Jean-Pierre Banâtre and Daniel Le Métayer introduced the Γ language, which models computation as the global evolution of a collection of values interacting freely. This idea can be explained intuitively through the chemical reaction metaphor:

– Programs work on a data structure defined as a multiset of atomic values that can be thought of as a chemical solution. The values are molecules "floating" freely in the solution.

– Programs specify chemical reactions through conditional reaction rules.

For example, to define the function that computes the maximum of a set of numbers, we can consider the numbers to be molecules in the solution, and the reaction is specified by the rule

$$(max) \quad x, y \to x \quad \text{if} \ \ x \geq y$$

This rule indicates that a reaction can take place between the molecules x and y, provided $x \geq y$, and as a result x and y are replaced by x.

In the solution, reactions can take place in parallel, provided the side condition of the reaction rule is satisfied. Since reactions can occur simultaneously in many points of the solution, this formalism allows us to model concurrent computations in a simple and concise way. For example, after repeated, possibly concurrent, applications of the rule (max) given above, there will be only one molecule in the solution, which is the maximum of the numbers originally in the solution. Note how compact this program is (just one line of code).

The Chemical abstract machine is an implementation of this paradigm of concurrency; it defines a concurrent programming methodology that is free from control management in the sense that the concurrent components (i.e., the molecules in this case) are freely moving in the solution and can communicate whenever they come in contact. It is possible to show that a calculus of concurrent communicating processes such as the one defined in the previous sections can be implemented via the Chemical abstract machine.

8.6 Further reading

The process calculus defined in this chapter is based on Robin Milner's CCS (a calculus of communicating systems) [33]. Several other calculi are available to specify and reason about concurrent processes; the references are numerous, but we mention in particular the π-calculus, developed also by Robin Milner as a direct generalisation of CCS that permits more flexible communication patterns [34]. For a detailed account of the theory of bisimulation, we refer to David Park's work [40]. An advanced treatment of the π-calculus theory can be found in [45]. For more information on the Γ formalism and the Chemical abstract machine, we recommend the articles [3, 5].

8.7 Exercises

1. Prove that the relation $\sim$ introduced in Definition 8.6 is an equivalence relation, as stated in Proposition 8.7.

2. Prove that if $p \sim q$, then p simulates q and q simulates p.

   The reverse is not true. Can you give a counterexample?

3. Show that the following definition is equivalent to the definition of strong bisimulation (see Definition 8.6):

   R is a strong bisimulation if pRq implies

   a) for all n and for all $a_1, \ldots, a_n \in Act$,

   $$p \longrightarrow^{a_1,\ldots,a_n} p' \;\Rightarrow\; \exists q' \mid q \longrightarrow^{a_1,\ldots,a_n} q' \text{ and } p'Rq'$$

   b) for all n and for all $a_1, \ldots, a_n \in Act$,

   $$q \longrightarrow^{a_1,\ldots,a_n} q' \;\Rightarrow\; \exists p' \mid p \longrightarrow^{a_1,\ldots,a_n} p' \text{ and } p'Rq'$$

   where $p \longrightarrow^{a_1,\ldots,a_n} p'$ denotes a sequence of transitions from p to p' labelled by the actions $a_1, \ldots, a_n$.

4. Consider a counter defined as a device that can hold a natural number, increment its value, or decrement it, but if the value of the counter is zero, decrementing it does not change the value of the counter. Write a process expression defining such a counter.

5. In order to prove that $P \equiv Q$ implies $P \sim Q$ as stated in the second part of Proposition 8.14, it is sufficient to show that the structural congruence $\equiv$ is a strong bisimulation. Can you prove this fact?

6. Let P be the process defined by the expression $\nu \, def \, . (K_1 | K_2 | K_3)$, where

$$
\begin{aligned}
K_1 &= f.a.\bar{d}.K_1 \\
K_2 &= d.b.\bar{e}.K_2 \\
K_3 &= \bar{f}.e.c.K_3
\end{aligned}
$$

and let H be the process defined by the equation

$$H \quad = \quad a.b.c.H$$

a) Give labelled transition systems for P and for H.

b) Show that $P \sim H$.

7. Consider the process defined by $D(b, b', e, e') = C\langle b, b', e, e'\rangle$, where C is the bidirectional channel defined in Example 8.15. Let the process CD be defined by

$$CD(a, a', e, e') = \nu bb'.(C\langle a, a', b, b'\rangle | D\langle b, b', e, e'\rangle)$$

Describe the transition diagram for CD, and show that CD can transmit messages like a bidirectional channel but can also be in deadlock.

9

Emergent Models of Computation

In this chapter, we briefly present two fields that have emerged in recent years: *natural computing* and *quantum computing*.

Natural computing refers to computational techniques inspired in part by systems occurring in nature. In particular, this includes models of computation that take inspiration from the mechanisms that take place in living organisms. The main observation here is that living organisms routinely perform complex processes at the micro-level in a way that is hard to emulate with standard computing technology. Several new models of computation have been proposed in recent years based on advances in biology that have allowed us to understand better how various processes take place. This family of computation models is generally known as *bio-computing*.

Quantum computing refers to computation that uses quantum technology. One of the motivations for the study of quantum computing stems from the current trend to miniaturise computers. It has been observed that if this trend continues, it will be necessary to replace the current technology with quantum technology, as on the atomic scale matter obeys the rules of quantum mechanics, which are very different from the classical rules. Indeed, quantum technology is already available (albeit not yet for general computer science applications), and it can offer much more than compact and fast computers: It can give rise to a new kind of programming paradigm based on quantum principles.

The following sections give a short introduction to these two computing paradigms.

9.1 Bio-computing

Biologically inspired models of computation make use of natural processes occurring in living organisms as a basis for the development of programming techniques. Since complex algorithms are efficiently performed at different levels in a living organism (in particular, at the cell level, at the gene level, and at the protein level), the idea is to develop algorithms to solve complex computational problems by applying similar techniques. This research problem should not be confused with the problem of developing software to simulate behaviours or processes that occur in nature (sometimes called "executable biology"). Although biological modelling is one of the applications of bio-computing, software tools to represent and analyse biological processes have been written in a variety of programming languages with different underlying computation models. Bio-computing, in the sense defined here, should also not be confused with the branch of computer science that studies the use of biological materials in hardware components.

The three main levels at which biological mechanisms occur correspond to biochemical networks, performing all the mechanical and metabolic tasks, formalised as protein interaction; gene regulatory networks, which control the activities by regulating the concentrations of proteins; and transport networks, defined in terms of biochemical compartments (or membranes) where protein interactions are confined. Accordingly, biologically inspired models of computation can be classified by taking into account the level at which they work.

Without going into the details, we will describe here the main features of two models of computation: membrane systems, introduced by Gheorghe Paun, which take inspiration from the transport networks, and the protein-centric interaction systems defined by Vincent Danos and Cosimo Laneve. These two computation models are representative of the two main classes of bio-computing formalisms, but we should point out that several other calculi have been proposed; this is an active research area and there is no "standard" model.

9.1.1 Membrane calculi

Membrane systems are a class of distributed, parallel computing devices inspired by the basic features of biological membranes, which are the essence of the transport networks. Membranes play a fundamental role in the complex reactions that take place in living organisms.

A membrane structure can be seen as a series of compartments where multisets of objects can be placed. Membranes are permeable, so objects can pass through a membrane and move between compartments. The membranes can change their permeability, and they can dissolve or divide, thus changing the geometrical configuration of the membrane structure. This definition is based on the observation that any biological system is a complex hierarchical structure where the flow of materials and information is essential to its function.

In membrane calculi, the objects inside the membranes evolve in accordance with reaction rules associated with the compartments. Reaction rules can be applied in a parallel, non-deterministic manner. In this way, computation can be defined as sequences of transitions between configurations of the system.

Programs in this formalism are called P systems. The objects (which are usually numbers or strings) are the data structures on which the program works. Many different classes of P systems have already been investigated, and, in particular, it has been shown that P systems are Turing complete: It is possible to encode a Turing machine using a P system.

Since P systems can perform parallel computations, we could use P programs to model concurrent systems. In fact, the reverse is also possible, and indeed process calculi have been used in the past to model biological mechanisms. For instance, variants of the π-calculus have been used to represent cellular processes. However, the use of more abstract systems, such as membrane calculi or protein-interaction calculi, has the advantage of permitting a more clear and concise representation of biological systems.

9.1.2 Protein interaction calculi

The use of process calculi to represent biological systems has led to the design of several different calculi. Here we briefly describe the κ-calculus, which is inspired by the mechanism of protein interaction. Our presentation will follow the graphical intuitions behind the calculus; there is also an algebraic presentation.

The protein interaction calculus, as its name indicates, places a strong emphasis on the notion of interaction. In this sense, this formalism is closely related to the interaction nets that were the subject of Chapter 7. One of the main differences is that the notion of interaction here is more abstract in the sense that interactions reflect protein behaviour and are therefore not restricted to binary interactions involving principal ports of agents as in the case of interaction nets.

Each protein has a structure that can be represented in an abstract way as a set of switches and binding sites, not all of them accessible at a given time. These components, generally called *domains*, determine possible bindings between proteins and, as a consequence, possible interactions. Interactions can result in changes in the protein folding, which in turn can affect the interaction capabilities of the protein. The notion of a *site* is used in the κ-calculus to abstract over domains and folding states of a protein. Sites may be *free* or bound, and the free sites can be *visible* or *hidden*.

In the graphical representation, proteins are nodes in the graph and sites are ports, where edges can be attached, but only if the site is free and visible. Bound sites correspond to sites that are already involved in a binding with another protein (i.e., ports where an edge has been attached).

The graphs obtained by combining several nodes (i.e., proteins) and their links are called *protein complexes* or simply complexes. In biological terms, the complexes represent groups of proteins connected together by low-energy bounds governed by protein-interaction rules. A collection of proteins and complexes is called a *solution*; solutions evolve by means of reactions. Computationally, solutions are graphs where rewriting can take place, as defined by graph-rewriting rules associated with the biochemical reactions.

Biochemical reactions are either *complexations* or *decomplexations*: A complexation is a reaction that creates a new complex out of proteins that can interact, whereas a decomplexation breaks a complex into smaller components. These reactions may occur in parallel and may involve activation or deactivation of sites. Causality does not allow simultaneous complexations and decomplexations at the same site. From a computational point of view, this means that not all graph rewriting rules can be accepted as biochemical reactions. For this reason, in the κ-calculus there are constraints on the kind of graph rewriting rules that can be defined as protein-interaction rules. For instance, the left-hand sides should be connected, and a new edge can be attached to a given site only if the site is free and visible.

Computationally, the κ-calculus is universal: Turing machines can be easily simulated in this calculus by representing the contents of the tape as a finite chain of nodes in the graph and using a system of graph rewriting rules to represent the transitions between configurations of the machine. Compilations of (the algebraic version of) the calculus into the π-calculus are also available.

9.2 Quantum computing

A quantum computer is a device that makes direct use of quantum mechanics in order to perform computations. Roughly, if we think of computation as the process of performing operations on data, the main difference between a classical computer and a quantum one lies in the physical laws that govern the medium used to store the data and the mechanisms used to manipulate the data. In quantum computers, quantum properties are used to represent data and perform operations on these data.

Before describing in more detail the principles behind quantum computing, we need to recall a few notions from quantum physics.

Around 1900, physicists such as Max Planck, Niels Bohr, Erwin Schrödinger, and others were working on a theory that became known as "quantum physics". The name derives from the word used by Planck when he announced that radiant energy could only be propagated in tiny, indivisible bundles called *quanta*. The word *photon* is used to refer to a quantum of light.

Quantum physics gives a description of the universe that is capable of explaining phenomena that cannot be explained by classical laws. One of the best-known examples is a simple experiment using a beam splitter with equal probability of reflecting or transmitting the photons (e.g., a half-silvered mirror). When a photon source is directed towards the beam splitter, according to the classical laws of physics, half of the photons should pass and half should be reflected. Indeed, this is what the experiment with one beam splitter shows. However, if instead of measuring the light that passes and the light that is reflected we use two full mirrors to reflect it back to a second beam splitter, as indicated in Figure 9.1, then the result does not agree with classical intuition. Instead of seeing photons again split equally, we see that all the photons end up in the same path (marked *result* in Figure 9.1).

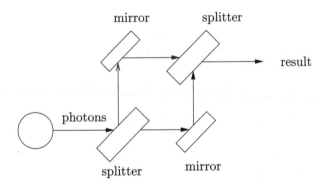

Figure 9.1 Two beam splitters.

The results of this experiment cannot be explained if we assume that after the photon encounters the first beam splitter it is either reflected or transmitted with equal probability, as classical laws indicate. However, it can be explained if we assume that the first beam splitter has caused the photon to be in a *superposition* of states (a combination of "reflected" and "transmitted"). Then, the second beam splitter applies the same transformation, causing the superposition to unfold into only one of the states.

The classical laws of physics are a good approximation of quantum mechanics at the macroscopic scale, but on the quantum level the classical laws are inaccurate, as this experiment shows, and the quantum laws should be used instead.

The main idea behind quantum computation is then to replace the classical circuits in traditional computers by quantum gates to obtain a computer whose work is quantum-mechanical.

The notion of a *quantum bit*, or *qubit*, is fundamental in quantum computing. A qubit can be encoded in a two-level system such as a photon. Thus, unlike classical bits, which represent binary information, in a quantum system the state of the qubit is generally defined by a vector in a two-dimensional Hilbert space. This is a combination of the basis vectors, usually written as $|0\rangle$ and $|1\rangle$ and corresponding to the classic binary values. In this way, it is possible to represent states with superposition. In general, a qubit's state can be written as

$$\alpha|0\rangle + \beta|1\rangle$$

where α and β are complex numbers such that $\alpha^2 + \beta^2 = 1$; states that differ only by a scalar factor with modulus 1 are considered indistinguishable.

One important difference between classic bits and qubits is the role of *measurement*. If a qubit is in the state $\alpha|0\rangle + \beta|1\rangle$, it means that its value, if measured, will be 0 with probability α^2 and 1 with probability β^2.

Another important difference is the *entanglement* phenomenon, which can arise in systems with two or more qubits. This means that the states of the qubits may be correlated in such a way that a measurement on one of the qubits will determine the result of the measurement in the other (even if the qubits are physically separated).

In a quantum circuit, logical qubits (quantum binary digits) are carried along "wires" and quantum gates act on the qubits, changing their state.

The first formal quantum circuit model was proposed by David Deutsch, who also defined a quantum Turing machine. Not only do these results show that quantum mechanics can be used to design computers, but also it has been shown that there are efficient algorithms to solve problems for which no efficient solution is known on a standard or probabilistic Turing machine. Thus, if large-scale quantum computers could be built, they would be able to solve certain problems, such as integer factorisation, much faster than any current classical computer. This has enormous implications in areas such as cryptography since many encryption protocols would then be easy to break.

Quantum computing is still in its early stages, but experiments have been carried out in which quantum computations were executed on a very small number of qubits. Research continues, and we can expect that new results will be available soon due to the important consequences of this research in areas such as cryptanalysis.

9.3 Further reading

For further information on quantum computing, we refer the reader to the introductory book by Kaye, Laflamme, and Mosca [26]; a survey on quantum programming languages can be found in [17].

The use of process calculi to represent biological systems has led to the design of several calculi. In addition to the membrane calculi and the κ-calculus discussed in this chapter, for which we refer the reader to Paun's work [41] and Danos and Laneve's article [11], respectively, we can mention the brane calculi designed by Luca Cardelli [8] and the biochemical machine (BIOCHAM) [14], amongst others.

10
Answers to Selected Exercises

Exercises in Chapter 1

1. Give more examples of total and partial functions on natural numbers.

   Answer:

   There are many examples of total functions. Addition, multiplication, and any combination of these, as well as the well-known factorial function, are all total. Subtraction is partial on natural numbers (but total on integers).

2. To test whether a number is even or odd, a student has designed the following function:

   $$test(x) \stackrel{\text{def}}{=} \quad \text{if } x = 0 \text{ then "even"}$$
   $$\text{else if } x = 1 \text{ then "odd" else } test(x\text{-}2)$$

   Is this a total function on the set of integer numbers? Is it total on the natural numbers?

   Answer:

   The set of natural numbers contains 0 and all the positive integers. For these, the test provided above gives a result: For 0 the result is "even", for 1 the result is "odd", and for any number x greater than 1 the number x-2 is still a natural number that can be tested again. Since each recursive call to the function test carries a smaller argument, it is easy to see that eventually the function will be called with either 0 or 1 and will produce a result. Therefore the function is total on natural numbers.

However, if the function is called with a negative number, for example test(-1), then there is no result. Therefore the function is partial on integers.

3. Consider the following variant of the Halting problem:

> Write an algorithm H such that, given the description of an algorithm A that requires one input, H will return 1 if A stops for any input I and H will return 0 if there is at least one input I for which A does not stop.

In other words, the algorithm H should read the description of A and decide whether it stops for all its possible inputs or there is at least one input for which A does not stop.

Show that this version of the Halting problem is also undecidable.

Answer:

We adapt the proof of undecidability given for the Halting problem in Section 1.2.

The specification of H indicates that $H(A) = 1$ if A stops for all inputs and $H(A) = 0$ if there is some I such that $A(I)\uparrow$.

Assuming H exists, we can build an algorithm C such that $C(A)\uparrow$ if $H(A) = 1$ and $C(A) = 0$ otherwise. In other words, $C(A)$ diverges if, for all inputs I, $A(I)$ stops; otherwise $C(A)$ stops.

Now, if we run C with argument C, we have

$C(C)\uparrow$ if and only if, for all inputs I, $C(I)$ stops.

This is a contradiction: If C stops with any input, this includes also the input C, and therefore $C(C)$ should stop.

Selected exercises from Chapter 2

2. Build finite automata with alphabet $\{0, 1\}$ to recognise

   a) the language of strings that have three consecutive 0s;

   b) the language of strings that do not have three consecutive 1s.

   Answer:

   The diagrams below specify the required automata.

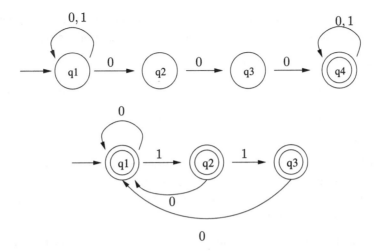

4. Let A be a finite automaton. Show that the set of subwords (that is, pre-fixes, suffixes, or any continuous segment) of the words in the language $L(A)$ can also be recognised by a finite automaton.

Answer:

To show that the language consisting of prefixes of words in $L(A)$ is recog-nisable by a finite automaton, we can simply build an automaton for it using as a starting point the automaton A. Indeed, to recognise a prefix of a word in $L(A)$, it is sufficient to turn every state in A for which there is a path to a final state into a final state. In this way, we have a finite automaton A' with the same alphabet as A and such that if a word is a prefix (i.e., the initial segment) of a word in $L(A)$, then A' will reach a final state.

Recognising suffixes is slightly more subtle, but again, starting from A we can build an automaton with the required property by inserting ϵ transitions between the initial state of A and all the other states for which there is a path to a final state. This gives a non-deterministic automaton A'' that, for any suffix (i.e., final segment) of a word in $L(A)$, reaches a final state.

Finally, combining both techniques, we can obtain an automaton that recog-nises any continuous segment of words in $L(A)$.

5. Use the Pumping Lemma to show that the language L containing all the words of the form $a^n b^n c^n$, for any $n \geq 0$, cannot be recognised by a finite automaton.

Answer:

Similar to Corollary 2.11. We sketch the idea: If a word $a^n b^n c^n$ is in L, then as a consequence of the Pumping Lemma there is a substring that can be repeated an arbitrary number of times. Therefore L contains strings where the number of symbols a, b, or c is different, which contradicts the assumptions.

6. How can a push-down automaton recognise the language

$$\{w\overline{w} \mid w \text{ is a string of 0s and 1s and } \overline{w} \text{ is its mirror image}\}?$$

Give an informal description of such an automaton.

Answer:

It is easy to build a non-deterministic automaton that recognises this language. The idea is to define states that non-deterministically put in the stack the symbols read and also start popping symbols in case we have already reached the middle point in the word.

7. Show that the class of languages recognisable by push-down automata (i.e., the class of context-free languages) is closed under union and concatenation but not under intersection.

Answer:

Union: Assume PDA_1 and PDA_2 recognise two context-free languages, L_1 and L_2. To build a PDA that recognises the union of L_1 and L_2, it is sufficient to include all the states in PDA_1 and PDA_2 (without loss of generality, we can assume that the sets of states are disjoint) but define a new initial state q_0 with ϵ transitions to the initial states of PDA_1 and PDA_2 (which are no longer initial states in the new automaton).

Concatenation: Similarly, we can build a PDA that recognises all the words formed by concatenation of a word from L_1 and a word from L_2 simply by adding ϵ transitions from the final states in PDA_1 (which are no longer final in the new automaton) to the initial state in PDA_2 (which is no longer an initial state).

Intersection: Showing that context-free languages are not closed by intersection is more difficult. To show it, we rely on the fact that the language consisting of all the strings of the form $a^n b^n c^n$ is not context-free (see Section 2.3 and Exercise 5 of Chapter 2). This language is the intersection of two context-free languages, $L_1 = \{a^* b^n c^n \mid n \geq 0\}$ and $L_2 = \{a^n b^n c^* \mid n \geq 0\}$, where a^* denotes a string with an arbitrary number (0 or more) of symbols a and c^* denotes a string with an arbitrary number (0 or more) of symbols c. We leave to the reader the proof that there are PDAs that recognise L_1 and L_2 — see the PDA defined in Section 2.3 to recognise the language

$$\{(^n)^n \mid n \text{ is a natural number}\}$$

8. Describe a Turing machine that recognises the language of the strings $w \bullet w$, where w is a string over an alphabet $\{0, 1\}$.

Answer:

The machine can be formally defined as follows:

- The set Q of states contains $q_0, q_1, q_2, q_3, q_4, q_5, q_6, q_{accept}, q_{reject}$.

  The initial state is q_0, and the final states are q_{accept} and q_{reject}.

- The input alphabet is $\{0, 1\}$. The tape alphabet contains additionally the blank symbol $\circ$.

- The transition function δ is defined by

$$\delta(q_0, \bullet) = (q_{accept}, \bullet, R)$$
$$\delta(q_0, 0) = (q_1, \circ, R) \qquad \delta(q_0, 1) = (q_4, \circ, R)$$
$$\delta(q_1, 0) = (q_1, 0, R) \qquad \delta(q_1, 1) = (q_1, 1, R)$$
$$\delta(q_1, \bullet) = (q_2, \bullet, R) \qquad \delta(q_2, \bullet) = (q_2, \bullet, R)$$
$$\delta(q_2, 0) = (q_3, \bullet, L) \qquad \delta(q_3, \bullet) = (q_3, \bullet, L)$$
$$\delta(q_3, 0) = (q_3, 0, L) \qquad \delta(q_3, 1) = (q_3, 1, L)$$
$$\delta(q_3, \circ) = (q_0, \circ, R) \qquad \delta(q_4, 0) = (q_4, 0, R)$$
$$\delta(q_4, 1) = (q_4, 1, R) \qquad \delta(q_4, \bullet) = (q_5, \bullet, R)$$
$$\delta(q_5, \bullet) = (q_5, \bullet, R) \qquad \delta(q_5, 1) = (q_6, \bullet, L)$$
$$\delta(q_6, \bullet) = (q_6, \bullet, L) \qquad \delta(q_6, 0) = (q_6, 0, L)$$
$$\delta(q_6, 1) = (q_6, 1, L) \qquad \delta(q_6, \circ) = (q_0, \circ, R)$$
$$\delta(q_i, x) = (q_{reject}, \circ, R) \qquad \text{for any } (q_i, x) \text{ not defined above}$$

The idea is that the machine, once started in the first symbol of the word, remembers whether it is a 0 or a 1 (by moving to q_1 or q_4) and replaces the first symbol by a blank. Then it jumps over all the remaining 0s and 1s until it finds a $\bullet$, and then it looks for the first symbol different from $\bullet$. If it is the required 0 or 1, then it replaces it by a $\bullet$ (otherwise, the word is rejected). After replacing the symbol by $\bullet$, the machine goes backwards to the beginning of the word and repeats the cycle.

Selected exercises from Chapter 3

3. Compute the normal forms of the following terms

   a) $\lambda y.(\lambda x.x)y$

   b) $\lambda y.y(\lambda x.x)$

c) II

d) KI

e) KKK

where $K = \lambda xy.x$ and $I = \lambda x.x$.

Answer:

We have the following reductions to normal form:

a) $\lambda y.(\lambda x.x)y \to \lambda y.y$

b) $\lambda y.y(\lambda x.x)$ (the term was already a normal form!)

c) $II = (\lambda x.x)(\lambda x.x) \to \lambda x.x = I$

d) $KI = (\lambda xy.x)(\lambda x.x) \to \lambda yx.x$

e) $KKK = ((\lambda xy.x)(\lambda xy.x))(\lambda xy.x) \to^* \lambda xy.x = K$ (recall that application associates to the left).

4. Different notions of normal form were discussed in Chapter 3, including the full normal form (or simply normal form) and weak head normal form.

   a) What is the difference between a term having a normal form and being a normal form? Write down some example terms.

   b) If a closed term is a weak head normal form, it has to be an abstraction $\lambda x.M$. Why?

   c) Indicate whether the following λ-terms have a normal form:

      – $(\lambda x.(\lambda y.yx)z)v$

      – $(\lambda x.xxy)(\lambda x.xxy)$

   d) Show that the term $\Omega = (\lambda x.xx)(\lambda x.xx)$ does not have a normal form. Find a term different from Ω that is not normalising (i.e., a term such that every reduction sequence starting from it is infinite).

Answer:

   a) A term is in normal form if it is irreducible (i.e., it has no β-redex). It has a normal form if it can be reduced to a term in normal form. For example, the term $(\lambda x.x)(\lambda x.x)$ has a normal form but is not a normal form.

   b) A weak head normal form is a term where all β-redexes occur under an abstraction. If a term is closed, it cannot be just a variable. It may be an application or an abstraction. In the latter case, it is a weak head normal form. We will now show that it cannot be an application. For this, we reason by contradiction. Suppose that the term is an application (MN). Since it is closed and it is a weak head normal form, M must be an application, $M = (M_1 \ldots M_2 \ldots M_n)$, where M_1 is either a variable or an abstraction. The first contradicts the closedness assumption, and the latter contradicts the assumption that the term is a weak head normal form.

c) The term $(\lambda x.(\lambda y.yx)z)v$ has a normal form. It reduces to zv, which is in normal form. The term $(\lambda x.xxy)(\lambda x.xxy)$, on the other hand, does not have a normal form.

d) The term Ω is reducible, but its only redex is Ω itself. If we reduce it, we again obtain Ω. Therefore, the only reduction sequence out of Ω is the infinite sequence $\Omega \to \Omega \to \Omega \ldots$.

Another example was given above: $(\lambda x.xxy)(\lambda x.xxy)$.

The term $(\lambda x.y)\Omega$ is interesting. It is not strongly normalisable since there is an infinite reduction sequence that always reduces the Ω subterm; however, it has a normal form since it reduces in one step to y. This is an example of a term that is normalisable but not strongly normalisable.

5. Explain why if a reduction system is confluent, then each term has at most one normal form.

Answer:

In a confluent reduction system, for any term M such that $M \to^* M_1$ and $M \to^* M_2$, there is some term M_3 such that $M_1 \to^* M_3$ and $M_2 \to^* M_3$. Now, let us assume, by contradiction, that in a confluent system some term M has two different normal forms, N_1 and N_2. Since the system is confluent, there must exist a term N_3 that joins N_1 and N_2. But then N_1 and N_2 are not normal forms since they reduce to N_3 (contradiction).

11. Combinatory logic (CL for short) is a universal model of computation. Terms in the language of CL are built out of variables $x, y, \ldots$, constants S and K, and applications $(M\ N)$. More precisely, terms are generated by the grammar

$$M, N ::= x \mid S \mid K \mid (M\ N)$$

The standard notational conventions are used to avoid brackets: Applications associate to the left, and we do not write the outermost brackets. For instance, we write $K\,x\,y$ for the term $((K\,x)\,y)$.

There are two computation rules in combinatory logic:

$$
\begin{aligned}
K\,x\,y &\ \to\ x \\
S\,x\,y\,z &\ \to\ x\,z\,(y\,z)
\end{aligned}
$$

a) Using the rules above, there is a sequence of reduction steps

$$SKKx \rightarrow^* x$$

Show all the reduction steps in this sequence.

b) The term SKK can be seen as the implementation of the identity function in this system since, for any argument x, the term $SKKx$ evaluates to x.

Show that SKM, where M is an arbitrary term, also defines the identity function.

c) Consider the system of combinatory logic without the second computation rule (that is, only the rule $Kxy \rightarrow x$ may be used). We call this weaker system CL^-.

We call CL^+ the system of combinatory logic with an additional constant I and rule $Ix \rightarrow x$.

Indicate whether each of the following statements is true or false and why.

    i. In CL^-, all the reduction sequences are finite.

    ii. The system CL^+ has the same computational power as the system CL.

    iii. The system CL^- is Turing complete.

Answer:

a) The reduction sequence is $SKKx \rightarrow Kx(Kx) \rightarrow x$.

b) The reduction $SKMx \rightarrow Kx(Mx) \rightarrow x$ justifies the claim.

c) This question has three parts. In the first part, the claim is that all reduction sequences are finite. This is true because each application of the reduction rule decreases the size of the term, and therefore reductions eventually terminate.

It is easy to see that CL^+ has the same computational power as CL since I can be implemented in CL as shown above.

On the other hand, CL^- is strictly less powerful than CL: CL^- is not Turing complete. Several arguments can be used to justify this claim: the fact that each reducible term is equivalent to one of its subterms, the fact that there is no way to copy arguments, the termination of the reduction relation, etc.

Selected exercises from Chapter 4

1. Show that the factorial function is primitive recursive.

   Answer:

   The factorial function can be defined using the primitive recursive scheme as

   $$\begin{aligned} \text{factorial}(0) &= \text{S}(0) \\ \text{factorial}(\text{S}(n)) &= g(\text{factorial}(n), n) \end{aligned}$$

   where the auxiliary function g multiplies the first argument by the successor of the second. The function g can be defined by the composition of the multiplication and addition functions:

   $$g(x, y) = \text{add}(\pi_1(x, y), \text{mul}(x, y))$$

2. Show that the function f used in Example 4.6, defined by $f(0) = 0$ and $f(\text{S}(n)) = 1$, is primitive recursive.

   Answer:

   The function f can be defined as

   $$\begin{aligned} f(0) &= 0 \\ f(\text{S}(n)) &= \text{one}(f(n), n) \end{aligned}$$

   where $\text{one}(x, y) = \text{S}(\text{zero}(x, y))$ and $\text{zero}(x, y) = 0$.

5. Indicate whether the following statements are true or false:

   a) All primitive recursive functions are total.

   b) All total computable functions are primitive recursive.

   c) All partial recursive functions are computable.

   d) All total functions are computable.

   Answer:

   The first claim is true and was proved in Chapter 4.

   The second claim is false since there are total functions that are not primitive recursive. Ackermann's function, given at the end of Section 4.1, is an example of a total but not primitive recursive function.

   The third claim is true. The class of partial recursive functions is equivalent to the class of functions that can be computed by Turing machines.

   The fourth claim is false. The function that solves the Halting problem is total, but it is not computable.

7. In functional languages, there is a primitive function `if-then-else` that we can use to define a function by cases, depending on a Boolean condition (see the case construction in Definition 4.7). Thus,

   `if x == 0 then 0 else x * y`

   will return 0 if the value of x is equal to 0 and will return the product of x and y otherwise.

   Assume the function `mult` on natural numbers is defined by

   $$\texttt{mult x y} \stackrel{\text{def}}{=} \texttt{if x == 0 then 0 else x * y}$$

   where == is the equality test. Assume that e_1 == e_2 is evaluated by reducing e_1 and e_2 to normal form and then comparing the normal forms.

   a) Is `mult` commutative over numbers; i.e., will `mult m n` and `mult n m` compute the same result for all numbers m and n?

   b) Let `infinity` be the function defined by

      $$\texttt{infinity} \stackrel{\text{def}}{=} \texttt{infinity + 1}$$

      What is the value of `mult infinity 0`?

      What is the value of `mult 0 infinity`?

   Answer:

   If both arguments of `mult` are numbers, then the comparison with 0 always produces a result, and therefore `mult` is commutative. If one of the arguments is 0, the result is 0; otherwise it is the result of $x * y$.

   However, for `mult infinity 0`, the evaluation process does not terminate. The value of `infinity` is undefined, and therefore the comparison with 0 does not return a result.

   For `mult 0 infinity`, the value is 0 and can be found with a strategy that uses normal order.

Selected exercises from Chapter 5

1. Assuming that A, B, C are atoms, which of the following clauses are Horn clauses?

   a) $\neg A$

   b) $A \lor B \lor \neg C$

c) $A \lor \neg A$

d) A

Answer:

The only clause that is not a Horn clause is the second one (it has two positive literals).

4. Give the most general unifier (if it exists) of the following atoms (recall that [1,2] is short for the list [1| [2| []]]):

a) append([1,2],X,U), append([Y|L],Z,[Y|R])

b) append([1,2],X,[0,1]), append([Y|L],Z,[Y|R])

c) append([],X,[0,1]), append([Y|L],Z,[Y|R])

d) append([],X,[0]), append([],[X|L],[Y])

Answer:

a) The most general unifier of the terms append([1,2],X,U) and append([Y|L],Z,[Y|R]) is $\{Y \mapsto 1, L \mapsto [2], Z \mapsto X, U \mapsto [1|R]\}$.

b) The terms append([1,2],X,[0,1]), append([Y|L],Z,[Y|R]) are not unifiable since we need $Y = 1$ and $Y = 0$ at the same time.

c) The terms append([],X,[0,1]), append([Y|L],Z,[Y|R]) are not unifiable since we cannot unify the empty list with a non-empty list.

d) The terms append([],X,[0]), append([],[X|L],[Y]) are not unifiable since we cannot unify X with [X|L] (occur-check).

6. Show that the resolvent of the clauses

P :- $A_1, \ldots, A_n$

and

:- $Q_1, \ldots, Q_m$

is also a Horn clause.

Answer:

By definition, each Horn clause contains zero or one positive literal. Resolving eliminates one literal Q_i and replaces it by $A_1, \ldots, A_n$, with a suitable substitution (which will only modify the terms inside the literals). Therefore the resolvent is still a Horn clause.

7. Consider the program

   ```
   nat(s(X)) :- nat(X).
   ```

   ```
   nat(0).
   ```

   and the query

   ```
   :- nat(Y).
   ```

   a) Describe the complete SLD-resolution tree for this query.

   b) Explain why Prolog will not find an answer for this query.

   c) Change the program so that Prolog can find an answer.

Answer:

The complete SLD-tree is

$$\text{nat(Y)}$$
$$\{Y \mapsto s(X_1)\}/ \ \backslash \{Y \mapsto 0\}$$
$$\text{nat}(X_1) \quad \Diamond$$
$$\{X_1 \mapsto s(X_2)\}/ \ \backslash \{X_1 \mapsto 0\}$$
$$\text{nat}(X_2) \quad \Diamond$$
$$\vdots$$

Prolog will not find an answer because first it explores the leftmost branch, which is infinite in this case. We need to change the order of the clauses:

```
nat(0).
```

```
nat(s(X)) :- nat(X).
```

12. A graph is a set $V = \{a, b, c, \ldots\}$ of vertices and a set $E \subseteq V \times V$ of edges. We use the binary predicate edge to represent the edges: edge(a,b) means that there is an edge from a to b. In a directed graph, the edges have a direction, so edge(a,b) is different from edge(b,a). We say that there is a *path* from a to b in a graph if there is a sequence of one or more edges that allows us to go from a to b.

    a) Write a logic program defining the predicate path.

    b) Write a query to compute all the directed paths starting from a in the graph.

    c) Write a query to compute all the directed paths in the graph.

Answer:

The following program defines the predicate path:

```
path(X,Y) :- edge(X,Y).

path(X,Y) :- edge(X,Z), path(Z,Y).
```

The following query computes the paths starting from a:

```
:- path(a,X).
```

The following query computes all the paths:

```
:- path(X,Y).
```

Selected exercises from Chapter 6

1. What is the fundamental difference between a method defined by $l = \varsigma(x)b$ in an object o and a function with argument x defined by the λ-term $\lambda(x)b$?

   Answer:

   In $l = \varsigma(x)b$, x is the *self* variable. It refers to the whole object where the method l is defined.

   We could simulate method invocation using function application. Assume we define an object $o = [l_i = \lambda(x_i)b_i^{i \in 1 \dots n}]$. Then we can replace the usual invocation rule

   $$o.l_j \longrightarrow b_j\{x_j \mapsto o\}$$

   by

   $$o.l_j \longrightarrow (\lambda(x_j)b_j)o$$

   Observe that $(\lambda(x_j)b_j)o \rightarrow b_j\{x_j \mapsto o\}$ as required.

3. Add a method *get* in the object *loc* defined in Example 6.8 to represent a memory location, so that the field *value* is accessed by *get*.

   Answer:

   $$\begin{aligned} loc \;=\; &[value = 0, \\ &set = \varsigma(x)\lambda(n)x.value := n, \\ &get = \varsigma(x)x.value] \end{aligned}$$

4. In a calculus that combines objects, functions, numbers, and arithmetic functions, we have defined the following object:

$$loc \quad = \quad [value = 0,$$
$$set = \varsigma(x)\lambda(n)x.value := n,$$
$$incr = \varsigma(x)x.value := x.value + 1]$$

a) Describe in your own words the behaviour of the methods set and $incr$.

b) Evaluate the terms (and show the reduction steps)

   i. $loc.set(1).set(3).value$

   ii. $loc.incr.value$

where loc is the object defined above.

Answer:

The method set stores a value in the field $value$, and $incr$ increases by one the number stored in $value$.

The reductions are

$$
\begin{aligned}
loc.set(1).set(3).value \quad &\rightarrow \quad ((\lambda(n)loc.value := n)1).set(3).value \\
&\rightarrow \quad (loc.value := 1).set(3).value \\
&\rightarrow \quad [value = 1, set = \varsigma(x)\lambda(n)x.value := n, \\
incr = \varsigma(x)x.value &:= x.value + 1].set(3).value \\
&\rightarrow \quad ((\lambda(n)loc'.value := n)3).value \\
&\rightarrow \quad (loc'.value := 3).value \\
&\rightarrow \quad [value = 3, set = \varsigma(x)\lambda(n)x.value := n, \\
&\qquad incr = \varsigma(x)x.value := x.value + 1].value \\
&\rightarrow \quad 3
\end{aligned}
$$

$$
\begin{aligned}
loc.incr.value \quad &\rightarrow \quad (loc.value := loc.value + 1).value \\
&\rightarrow \quad (loc.value := 0 + 1).value \\
&\rightarrow \quad [value = 0 + 1, set = \varsigma(x)\lambda(n)x.value := n, \\
&\qquad incr = \varsigma(x)x.value := x.value + 1].value \\
&\rightarrow \quad 0 + 1 \rightarrow 1
\end{aligned}
$$

6. Recall the translation function $\mathcal{T}$ from the λ-calculus to the ς-calculus defined in Chapter 6:

$$\mathcal{T}(x) = x$$
$$\mathcal{T}(\lambda x.M) = [arg = \varsigma(x)x.arg, val = \varsigma(x)\mathcal{T}(M)\{x \mapsto x.arg\}]$$
$$\mathcal{T}(MN) = (\mathcal{T}(M).arg := \mathcal{T}(N)).val$$

a) Using this definition, write down the ς-terms obtained by the following translations:

   i. $T(\lambda x.x)$

   ii. $T(\lambda xy.x)$

   iii. $T(\lambda y.(\lambda x.x)y)$

   iv. $T((\lambda x.x)(\lambda y.y))$

b) Reduce $T((\lambda x.x)(\lambda y.y))$ to normal form using the reduction rules of the ς-calculus.

c) What are the advantages and disadvantages of a computation model that combines the ς-calculus and additional rewriting rules? Compare it with the pure ς-calculus.

Answer:

$$T(\lambda x.x) = [arg = \varsigma(x)x.arg, val = \varsigma(x)x.arg]$$

To compute $T(\lambda xy.x)$, we proceed as follows:

$$
\begin{aligned}
T(x) &= x \\
T(\lambda y.x) &= [arg = \varsigma(y)y.arg, val = \varsigma(y)x] \\
T(\lambda xy.x) &= [arg = \varsigma(x)x.arg, \\
& \qquad val = \varsigma(x)[arg = \varsigma(y)y.arg, val = \varsigma(y)x.arg]]
\end{aligned}
$$

To compute $T(\lambda y.(\lambda x.x)y)$, we proceed as follows:

$$
\begin{aligned}
T((\lambda x.x)y) &= ([arg = \varsigma(x)x.arg, val = \varsigma(x)x.arg].arg := y).val \\
T(\lambda y.(\lambda x.x)y) &= [arg = \varsigma(y)y.arg, \\
& \qquad val = \varsigma(y)([arg = \varsigma(x)x.arg, \\
& \qquad\qquad val = \varsigma(x)x.arg].arg := y.arg).val]
\end{aligned}
$$

Below we compute $T((\lambda x.x)(\lambda y.y))$ and reduce it to normal form.

$$
\begin{aligned}
T((\lambda x.x)(\lambda y.y)) &= ([arg = \varsigma(x)x.arg, val = \varsigma(x)x.arg].arg := \\
& \qquad [arg = \varsigma(y)y.arg, val = \varsigma(y)y.arg]).val \\
&\longrightarrow [arg = [arg = \varsigma(y)y.arg, val = \varsigma(y)y.arg], \\
& \qquad val = \varsigma(x)x.arg].val \\
&\longrightarrow [arg = [arg = \varsigma(y)y.arg, val = \varsigma(y)y.arg], \\
& \qquad val = \varsigma(x)x.arg].arg \\
&\longrightarrow [arg = \varsigma(y)y.arg, val = \varsigma(y)y.arg] \\
&= T(\lambda y.y)
\end{aligned}
$$

The advantages of a model of computation combining the ς-calculus with additional reduction rules include the fact that additional rules can make it easier to write programs in specific domains; for instance, an extension with the λ-calculus allows the natural representation of functional components of a program, specifically input/output.

The disadvantage is that an extension may break some useful properties (e.g., confluence).

7. Indicate whether each of the following statements about the ς-calculus is true or false and why.

   a) The ς-calculus is confluent; therefore each expression has at most one normal form in this calculus.

   b) The ς-calculus does not have an operation to add methods to an object; therefore it is not a Turing-complete model of computation.

Answer:

It is confluent, and confluence implies the unicity of normal forms.

It does not have an operation to extend objects with new methods, but it is Turing complete. For instance, the λ-calculus can be encoded in the object calculus, as shown in Chapter 6.

Selected exercises from Chapter 7

4. a) Give an interaction system to compute the Boolean function *and*.

   Answer:

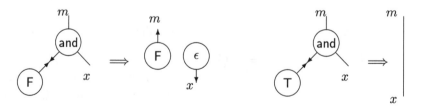

   b) Draw the interaction net representing the expression

$$(True \ and \ False) \ and \ True$$

   How many reductions are needed to fully normalise this net?

Answer:

We omit the diagram; the net has an active pair T ⋈ and, which creates another active pair F ⋈ and. This interaction produces an agent F and creates an active pair T ⋈ ε. The final result, after three interaction steps, is False.

6. Textual rules defining addition were given in Example 7.14. Can you write the textual version of the rules for multiplication given in Section 7.2?

Answer:

$$m(0, \epsilon) \qquad \bowtie \quad 0$$
$$m(x, \delta(y, z)) \quad \bowtie \quad S(m(\text{add}(x, z), y))$$

7. Explain why interaction nets are not suitable as a model for non-deterministic computations.

Answer:

Interaction nets are intrinsically deterministic. They are strongly confluent, which means that all reduction sequences produce the same result.

Selected exercises from Chapter 8

1. Prove that the relation $\sim$ introduced in Definition 8.6 is an equivalence relation, as stated in Proposition 8.7.

Answer:

Recall that $p \sim q$ if there is a strong bisimulation S such that (p, q) is in S. The relation S is a strong bisimulation if both S and S^{-1} are strong simulations.

To prove that $\sim$ is an equivalence relation, we need to show:

- Reflexivity: For all $p \in Q$, $p \sim p$.

  This can be proved using the relation S that contains all the pairs (p, p) such that p is a state in Q.

  The relations S and S^{-1} coincide in this case, and it is easy to see that S is a strong simulation.

- Symmetry: For all $p, q \in Q$, if $p \sim q$, then $q \sim p$.

  Note that $p \sim q$ implies that (p, q) is in a strong bisimulation S, and (q, p) is in S^{-1}, which is also a strong bisimulation by the definition of $\sim$. Hence $q \sim p$.

– Transitivity: For all $p, q, r \in Q$, if $p \sim q$ and $q \sim r$, then $p \sim r$.

To show transitivity, it is sufficient to prove that if S and S' are strong bisimulations, then so is $S \circ S'$, where

$$S \circ S' = \{(p, r) \mid (p, q) \in S \text{ and } (q, r) \in S' \text{ for some } q\}$$

2. Prove that if $p \sim q$, then p simulates q and q simulates p.

The reverse is not true. Can you give a counterexample?

Answer:

If $p \sim q$, then there is a strong bisimulation S such that pSq. By definition, this means that S and S^{-1} are strong simulations and contain the pairs (p, q) and (q, p), respectively. Therefore q simulates p and p simulates q.

The reverse implication is not true, as the following counterexample shows.

Consider two labelled transition systems, $D_1 = (Q_1, T_1)$ and $D_2 = (Q_2, T_2)$, such that in D_1 there is a state p with transitions $p \longrightarrow^a p_1$ and also $p \longrightarrow^a p'_1$; that is, from the state p, we can pass to the state p_1 or p'_1 (non-deterministically) by a. Assume that a further transition is possible from p_1 to p_2, labelled by b: $p_1 \longrightarrow^b p_2$.

Assume $Q_2 = \{q, q_1, q_2\}$ and T_2 contains the transitions $q \longrightarrow^a q_1$ and $q_1 \longrightarrow^b q_2$.

We can show that q simulates p using the relation

$$S = \{(p, q), (p_1, q_1), (p'_1, q_1), (p_2, q_2)\}$$

which is a strong simulation.

We can also show that p simulates q using the strong simulation

$$S' = \{(q, p), (q_1, p_1), (q_2, p_2)\}$$

However, S and S' are not inverses, and it is not possible to define a strong simulation such that the inverse is also a strong simulation because p and q are not observationally equivalent: There is a transition $p \longrightarrow^a p'_1$ after which D_1 is blocked (no further transitions are possible), whereas for D_2 there is no equivalent state.

4. Consider a counter defined as a device that can hold a natural number, increment its value, or decrement it, but if the value of the counter is zero, decrementing it does not change the value of the counter. Write a process expression defining such a counter.

Answer:

We can specify the counter using a transition system with a state for each possible value of the counter (for instance, $Q = C_n \ (n \geq 0)$) and transitions labelled by $incr$ or $decr$ to increment or decrement the value of the counter.

The following equations can be used to define the states:

$$\begin{aligned} C_0(inc, dec) &= inc.C_1\langle inc, dec\rangle + dec.C_0\langle inc, dec\rangle \\ C_{n+1}(inc, dec) &= inc.C_{n+2}\langle inc, dec\rangle + dec.C_n\langle inc, dec\rangle \end{aligned}$$

We initialise the counter by defining $Counter = C_0\langle inc, dec\rangle$.

5. In order to prove that $P \equiv Q$ implies $P \sim Q$ as stated in the second part of Proposition 8.14, it is sufficient to show that the structural congruence $\equiv$ is a strong bisimulation. Can you prove this fact?

Answer:

First, note that $\equiv$ and $\equiv^{-1}$ coincide, so we just need to show that $\equiv$ is a strong simulation.

Assume $P \equiv Q$. Then, if $P \longrightarrow^\alpha P'$, also $Q \longrightarrow^\alpha P'$, and $P' \equiv P'$ as required.

6. Let P be the process defined by the expression $\nu \ d \ e \ f.(K_1|K_2|K_3)$, where

$$\begin{aligned} K_1 &= f.a.\bar{d}.K_1 \\ K_2 &= d.b.\bar{e}.K_2 \\ K_3 &= \bar{f}.e.c.K_3 \end{aligned}$$

and let H be the process defined by the equation

$$H = a.b.c.H$$

a) Give labelled transition systems for P and for H.

b) Show that $P \sim H$.

Answer:

a) The set of states is isomorphic to the set of subexpressions. The transitions are defined by

$$\begin{aligned} P \longrightarrow^\tau \ & P^1 = \nu \ d \ e \ f.(a\bar{d}.K_1|db\bar{e}.K_2|ec.K_3) \\ \longrightarrow^a \ & P^2 = \nu \ d \ e \ f.(\bar{d}.K_1|db\bar{e}.K_2|ec.K_3) \\ \longrightarrow^\tau \ & P^3 = \nu \ d \ e \ f.(K_1|b\bar{e}.K_2|ec.K_3) \\ \longrightarrow^b \ & P^4 = \nu \ d \ e \ f.(K_1|\bar{e}.K_2|ec.K_3) \\ \longrightarrow^\tau \ & P^5 = \nu \ d \ e \ f.(K_1|K_2|c.K_3) \\ \longrightarrow^c \ & P \end{aligned}$$

and

$$H \longrightarrow^a H' = bc.H \longrightarrow^b H'' = c.H \longrightarrow^c H$$

To show that they are bisimilar, we can use the relation

$$S = \{(H, P), (H, P^1), (H', P^2), (H', P^3), (H'', P^4), (H'', P^5)\}.$$

Bibliography

[1] M. Abadi and L. Cardelli. *A Theory of Objects*. Monographs in Computer Science. Springer, 1996.

[2] S. Alves, M. Fernández, M. Florido, and I. Mackie. Linear recursive functions. In *Rewriting, Computation and Proof: Essays Dedicated to Jean-Pierre Jouannaud on the Occasion of His 60th Birthday*, volume 4600 of *Lecture Notes in Computer Science, Festchrift*. Springer, 2007.

[3] J.-P. Banâtre and D. Le Métayer. The GAMMA model and its discipline of programming. *Science of Computer Programming*, 15:55–77, 1990.

[4] H. P. Barendregt. *The Lambda Calculus: Its Syntax and Semantics*. North-Holland, 1984. Revised edition.

[5] G. Berry and G. Boudol. The Chemical Abstract Machine. In *Proceedings, 17th ACM Symposium on Principles of Programming Languages*, pages 81–94. ACM Press, 1990.

[6] R. Bird. *Introduction to Functional Programming Using Haskell*. Prentice-Hall, 1998.

[7] P. Blackburn, J. Bos, and K. Striegnitz. *Learn Prolog Now*, volume 7 of *Texts in Computing*. College Publications, 2007.

[8] L. Cardelli. Brane calculi — interactions of biological membranes. In *Computational Methods in Systems Biology: International Conference CMSB 2004*, volume 3082 of *Lecture Notes in Computer Science*, pages 257–280. Springer, 2005.

[9] A. Compagnoni and M. Fernández. An object calculus with algebraic rewriting. In *Programming Languages: Implementations, Logics, and Pro-*

grams. Proceedings of PLILP'97, volume 1292 of *Lecture Notes in Computer Science*. Springer, 1997.

[10] G. Cousineau and M. Mauny. *The Functional Approach to Programming.* Cambridge University Press, 1998.

[11] V. Danos and C. Laneve. Formal molecular biology. *Theoretical Computer Science*, 325(1):69–110, 2004.

[12] N. Dershowitz and Y. Gurevich. A natural axiomatization of computability and proof of Church's thesis. *Bulletin of Symbolic Logic*, 14(3):299–350, 2008.

[13] ECMA. ECMAScript language specification, 1999. Available from http://www.ecma.ch/ecma1/stand/ecma-262.htm.

[14] F. Fages and S. Soliman. Formal cell biology in BIOCHAM (tutorial). In *8th International School on Formal Methods for the Design of Computer, Communication and Software Systems: Computational Systems Biology. In memory of Nadia Busi*, volume 5016 of *Lecture Notes in Computer Science*. Springer, 2008.

[15] M. Fernández. *Programming Languages and Operational Semantics: An Introduction*, volume 1 of *Texts in Computing*. King's College Publications, 2004.

[16] M. Fernández and I. Mackie. A calculus for interaction nets. In G. Nadathur, editor, *Proceedings of the International Conference on Principles and Practice of Declarative Programming (PPDP'99)*, volume 1702 of *Lecture Notes in Computer Science*, pages 170–187. Springer-Verlag, 1999.

[17] S. J. Gay. Quantum programming languages: Survey and bibliography. *Mathematical Structures in Computer Science*, 16(4):581–600, 2006.

[18] M. Gladstone. A reduction of the recursion scheme. *Journal of Symbolic Logic*, 32:505–508, 1967.

[19] M. Gladstone. Simplification of the recursion scheme. *Journal of Symbolic Logic*, 36:653–665, 1971.

[20] J. Gosling, B. Joy, and G. Steele. *The Java Language Specification.* Addison-Wesley, 1996.

[21] C. Hankin. *An Introduction to Lambda Calculi for Computer Scientists*, volume 2 of *Texts in Computing*. King's College Publications, 2004.

[22] D. Harel and Y. A. Feldman. *Algorithmics: The Spirit of Computing.* Pearson Education, 2004.

[23] C. J. Hogger. *Introduction to Logic Programming*. APIC Studies in Data Processing. Academic Press, 1984.

[24] J. E. Hopcroft, R. Motwani, and J. D. Ullman. *Introduction to Automata Theory, Languages and Computability*. Addison-Wesley, 2000.

[25] D. H. H. Ingalls. Design principles behind Smalltalk. *BYTE Magazine*, 1981.

[26] P. Kaye, R. Laflamme, and M. Mosca. *An Introduction to Quantum Computing*. Oxford University Press, 2007.

[27] S. C. Kleene. *Introduction to Metamathematics*. North-Holland, 1952.

[28] Y. Lafont. Interaction nets. In *Proceedings, 17th ACM Symposium on Principles of Programming Languages*, pages 95–108. ACM Press, 1990.

[29] Y. Lafont. Interaction combinators. *Information and Computation*, 137(1):69–101, 1997.

[30] X. Leroy, D. Doligez, J. Garrigue, and J. Vouillon. The Objective Caml System. Technical report, INRIA.

[31] A. Martelli and U. Montanari. An efficient unification algorithm. *Transactions on Programming Languages and Systems*, 4(2):258–282, 1982.

[32] J. McCarthy, P. Abrahams, D. Edwards, T. Hart, and M. Levin. *LISP 1.5 Programmer's Manual, second edition*. MIT Press, 1965.

[33] R. Milner. *Communication and Concurrency*. Prentice-Hall, 1989.

[34] R. Milner. *Communicating and Mobile Systems: The π-Calculus*. Cambridge University Press, 1999.

[35] R. Milner, M. Tofte, and R. Harper. *The Definition of Standard ML*. MIT Press, 1990.

[36] J. C. Mitchell. *Concepts in Programming Languages*. Cambridge University Press, 2003.

[37] H. R. Nielson and F. Nielson. *Semantics with Applications: An Appetizer*. Undergraduate Topics in Computer Science. Springer, 2007.

[38] M. Odersky. Programming in Scala, 2005. Available from http://scala.epfl.ch/docu/.

[39] P. Odifreddi. *Classical Recursion Theory*. Elsevier Science, 1999.

[40] D. M. Park. Concurrency on automata and infinite sequences. In P. Deussen, editor, *Conference on Theoretical Computer Science*, volume 104 of *Lecture Notes in Computer Science*. Springer-Verlag, 1981.

[41] G. Paun. Computing with membranes. *Journal of Computer and System Sciences*, 61:108–143, 2000.

[42] J. S. Pinto. Sequential and concurrent abstract machines for interaction nets. In J. Tiuryn, editor, *Proceedings of Foundations of Software Science and Computation Structures (FOSSACS)*, volume 1784 of *Lecture Notes in Computer Science*, pages 267–282. Springer-Verlag, 2000.

[43] J. A. Robinson. A machine-oriented logic based on the resolution principle. *Journal of the ACM*, 12(1):23–41, 1965.

[44] P. Roussel. PROLOG: Manuel de référence et d'utilisation, 1975. Research Report, Artificial Intelligence Team, University of Aix-Marseille, France.

[45] D. Sangiorgi and D. Walker. *The π-Calculus: A Theory of Mobile Processes*. Cambridge University Press, 2001.

[46] J. Shoenfield. *Recursion Theory*. Springer-Verlag, 1993.

[47] M. Sipser. *Introduction to the Theory of Computation*. Course Technology — Cengage Learning, 2006.

[48] B. Stroustrup. *The C++ Programming Language*. Addison-Wesley Longman, 1997.

[49] T. Sudkamp. *Languages and Machines: An Introduction to the Theory of Computer Science*. Addison-Wesley, 2006.

[50] G. Sussman and G. Steele. Scheme: An interpreter for extended lambda calculus, 1975. MIT AI Memo 349.

[51] S. Thompson. *The Craft of Functional Programming*. Addison-Wesley, 1999.

[52] D. Ungar and R. B. Smith. Self: The power of simplicity. In N. K. Meyrowitz, editor, *Conference on Object-Oriented Programming Systems, Languages, and Applications (OOPSLA'87), 1987, Orlando, Florida, Proceedings*, SIGPLAN Notices 22(12), pages 227–242. ACM Press, 1987.

[53] G. Winskel. *The Formal Semantics of Programming Languages*. Foundations of Computing. MIT Press, 1993.

Index